MAKE YOUR OWN ANTIQUES

MAKE YOUR OWN ANTIQUES

by Francis W. Hagerty

Little, Brown and Company — Boston — Toronto

FIRST EDITION

T 10/75

The illustrations on pages 7 and 9 are reproduced courtesy of the U.S. Forest Products Laboratory.

LIBRARY OF CONGRESS CATALOGING IN PUBLICATION DATA

Hagerty, Francis.
    Make your own antiques.

    Bibliography: p.
    1. Furniture making—Amateurs' manuals. 2. Furniture, Colonial—United States. I. Title.
TT195.H33   749   75-19448
ISBN 0-316-33783-8

Design by Barbara Bell Pitnof

Published simultaneously in Canada
by Little, Brown & Company (Canada) Limited

PRINTED IN THE UNITED STATES OF AMERICA

To Mary, who helped make an idea a reality

Acknowledgments

My sincere thanks go to Arnold Weeks, whose unending enthusiasm and constructive criticism have made this book possible. Special thanks, too, go to Deane Lent, whose precise pen-and-ink drawings have brought alive the pieces exhibited on the back pages.

Contents

Contents

Foreword

Few individuals in these late years of the twentieth century see a job through from start to finish. The things we use every day are mass-produced in factories that rely increasingly on advanced technologies, automation, and the magical computer. There is no satisfying participation in the processes, and there is a resulting alienation from the things that are important to our lives. Many thoughtful observers have commented on the lack of satisfaction of modern man with this state of affairs. In these troubled times with the menace of an atomic holocaust, many search the past seeking a lost tranquillity and stability, for something less hectic than the modern pace — for roots. We are preoccupied with the ever new: new materials, new tools, new methods, new designs. We are liable to overlook things of the past as antiquated and unworthy of our notice. We should certainly acknowledge the many good things of the present and look to more in the future, but not to the exclusion of the good things of the past. "Good things of the past" holds for early American furniture, and this book presents an opportunity to participate by reproducing a selection of pine pieces from private and museum collections.

There is a poetry in this undertaking. A flow of associations on wood brings up folk memories of the forest. Here are lore and legend. The Indians dwelt in the forest; it was sanctuary and the source of useful materials. The English settler depended on the forest for lumber, firewood, and many articles in common use. We envision the farmer-craftsman in a shavings-strewn shop redolent of pine, at work making chairs, tables, and the needful in household gear.

Here the author offers the individual that rare satisfaction which comes of fashioning something with the hands using a few traditional tools and the table saw, a concession to modernity. The material is the wood of the native eastern white pine and maple, once abundant and still plentiful. These were used by the early farmer-craftsman and were admirably suited to his skills and needs. Good old pieces have stood the test of generations of use in material, style, and in construction. There is no other way to derive a full appreciation of the accomplishments of the old-time woodworker than to follow in his steps.

Francis Hagerty's enthusiasm for his subject fires the reader to get down to work. Here are lucid explanations of the best in shop practice, advice on how to select stock, what tools to acquire and where to buy them, much about finishes, and graphic, measured drawings. Here is the amateur's vademecum full of information that could be acquired only as

Foreword

an apprentice to a master in these arts — and this is Francis Hagerty, connoisseur and craftsman.

WILLIAM HENRY HARRISON
Director
Fruitlands Museums
Harvard, Massachusetts

January 1975

MAKE YOUR OWN ANTIQUES

Why Reproductions?

I AM WRITING the history of our people as written into things their hands made and used," said Henry Ford in 1929 at the opening of his museum in Dearborn, Michigan.

If he had in mind that pieces of his seventeenth-century "country furniture" would be appreciated and even copied by twentieth-century professional craftsmen as a native art form, he would be somewhat disappointed.

All too often the term "colonial American" has been grossly misused. In furniture stores across the country one sees it used irreverently in an attempt to apply an aura of respectability to bland or poor contemporary design. What tasteless creations are fashioned in maple, bathed in a finish of flyspeck brown, and sold to a confused public as early American or, even more ambiguously, as "contemporary colonial." Fabric-covered foam rubber cushions and forests of spindles that make up a hearthside "colonial" love seat are the result of some heady twentieth century scheme that never was true. What is to be gained by altering the stately lines of originals and, with obvious infidelity, then selling them as reproductions?

Few will debate the present-day aesthetic appeal of knotty pine either in paneling or in a sideboard, but to attribute to it an aura of eighteenth-century authenticity for use other than in housing or barn siding is pure nonsense. Pine was so plentiful along the East Coast two hundred years ago that boards free of knots were far more logical to use for paneling and furniture since they were structurally superior. The term "colonial knotty pine" was spawned and sponsored by promotion-minded furniture manufacturers. This mythical term came into being because the once abundant wide, clear boards were becoming increasingly difficult to find. A logical replacement is narrow pine lumber free of knots that can be edge-glued into wide panels. These wide boards, when properly stained and finished, simulate the once plentiful "pumpkin pine"; they are easy to make even in the home workshop.

Fortunately, "all of the people are not fooled all of the time," and a reverent appreciation of the designs and joinery of our forebears is very much in evidence in many amateur workshops throughout the country.

Thanks to foundations like the Ford Museum, New York's Metropolitan Museum, Sturbridge Village, Hartford's Wadsworth Atheneum, Boston's Museum of Fine Arts, and the Fruitlands Museums, to name a few, the public is being educated to recognize and appreciate the value of these colonial American creations. The "country furniture" in pumpkin pine and maple that they display and that is shown here reflects the creative art of the young

Why Reproductions?

nation that produced it long before man's technological "advances" changed his attitudes and his desires.

Only men of patience and inventiveness could have executed such practical art forms with the simplest of tools. The designs in this book were born in a far less complex period of history when individuality and accomplishment were not only tolerated but cherished.

Today collectors of Americana and a good segment of the public in general recognize the value of authentic reproductions. Properly executed, they are a source of admiration and pleasure for thousands of Americans who cannot take advantage of a good buy at a country auction — if one still exists.

Simple New England pine and maple furniture has much in common with contemporary living because it was designed to be functional and to fit into rooms of limited space. It obviously reflects the creative imagination of people imbued with a spirit of newly-won freedom.

At a time when each of us is becoming increasingly aware of his impersonal relationship with the vast American industrial machine, we look more than ever to the past for a feeling of stability and security. A marked increase in attendance at historical shrines and museums attests to our misgivings about the values of the present as we look longingly to the values of our ancestors.

Interest in these artifacts is often prompted by the vision, partly mythical and partly real, that our forefathers enjoyed the "good life" and controlled their own destinies — in spite of the fact that hindsight often ignores the realities of puritanical rule and the constant threats of disease and Indian invasion. Yet, if we listen intently, we'll hear the sweet sound of the broadax ringing in the winter forest whose echoes over the years remind us of the real truth: that America was built by the sweat of individuals, each of whom had his own reason for risking his life in a hostile environment.

It is in the creations of these individuals — their homes, their furnishings, their art — that we can see reflected the true spirit of their times. Often lacking satisfactory adhesives, colonial "joyners" ignored the limitation and fashioned sturdy chairs using both seasoned and unseasoned maple; as the freshly turned legs dried with time, they held in vicelike grip the dried or seasoned cross stretchers. And, too, these aesthetically pleasing pieces were made with tools so simple we now label them "primitive."

By reproducing their designs, we can see why they chose pumpkin pine for chair seats.

Why Reproductions?

They knew it was stronger for its weight than iron and easy to carve. In copying these old pieces, we are able to achieve a real feeling for the resourcefulness and native ingenuity that lie buried underneath the patina of centuries.

While many fine books have been written relating to the furniture of early America, few have acted as a guide to the purchase of the practical tools and the raw materials originally used in building these pieces. Easy-to-follow plans are of little use to the amateur if he does not know how and where to begin. Many hobbyists cannot afford the luxury of a well-equipped shop, and few realize the pitfalls which lie ahead in trying to find the correct tools and the wood with which to work.

This book is a treatise on the satisfaction to be gained from reproducing, in one's own home, pieces of colonial furniture of good original design that are as practical today as they were two hundred years ago. Its purpose is also to give the reader a knowledge of the materials used by our forebears together with an understanding of tools and the techniques for using them. It is a catalyst between the individual with a desire to make authentic early American reproductions and his creation of the finished piece. These reproductions will be as respectable and as honest in detail as their creator wishes them to be. These designs defy "improvement." To adapt or seriously alter them would be to dispel their charm.

While learning how these pieces were created and the proper use of hand tools in copying them, we shall sharpen unknown skills that are latent in us.

It is hoped that these pages will open new fields of interest to men and women who in the past have felt that a cabinetmaker's skill is necessary to achieve the satisfaction of creating functional and admirable furniture. Certainly, he who makes his own is twice rewarded. The joy of creation is surpassed only by the thrill of having one's own handiwork taken for a two-hundred-year-old original.

A Word on Wood

THIS COAST is mountainous and isles of huge rocks are overgrown for most part, with most sorts of excellent good woods for building houses, boats, barks or ships," noted Captain John Smith in 1614 as he wrote his impressions while coasting northward along the New England shores.

The endless virgin forest that once blanketed the coastal areas was a dense, almost impenetrable barrier that seemed to extend to Asia. This wilderness, with its seemingly limitless stands of timber, was under the relentless attack of the woodsman's ax even as Captain Smith was writing in his log. It was this tool with which the settlers built America.

It did not take them long. In November, when the little *Fortune* set sail on her return voyage to England, she was "laden with good clapboards as full as she could stowe" presumably riven from huge clear "punkin" pine logs with wedge, froe and maul.*

In the heart of the deep and damp forests grew the stately eastern white pines that frequently grew to heights of two hundred and fifty feet and more. They grew with the straightness of an arrow and with shafts of one hundred feet entirely free of limbs. The wood of these slow-growing giants was clear and soft and it had the yellowish color of the meat of the pumpkin. For this reason, the early settler referred to it as "pumpkin" pine.†

The forest was a source of shelter, food, medicine, tools, and wagons for the settler. He used charcoal in prodigious amounts to smelt bog iron to fashion his axes. He used wood to build his home and heat it. He fashioned from wood the spinning wheel on which his wife spun the yarn for his clothing. Wood made the plow with which he tilled the soil. The forests supplied the humble stump fences that contained the vital livestock. These huge mats of roots, often eight to ten feet in diameter and laboriously wrenched from the earth by man and ox, were turned on edge to surround the pastureland. "Hardly a man is now alive who remembers" the sculptured tracery of these roots washed, tinted, and smoothed by hundreds of years of rain and sun.

By trial and error he learned that this white pine, when properly dried, was a blessing in many ways. He cut and shaped it with greater ease than any other structural material. He used it extensively for beams, posts, and framework in building houses, barns, and bridges. Its great insulating properties made it ideal boarding for the house and barn; it was an effective barrier against the bitter cold of winter and the heat of summer. Because

* John Gardner, "The Little Known Ship Axe," *National Fisherman*, April, 1973.
† George Emerson, *A Report on Trees and Shrubs in the Forest of Massachusetts*, Boston: Little, Brown, 1875.

A Word on Wood

of its great resistance to rot and weathering, he used it almost exclusively in making clap-boarding, shingles, and window sash. Because of the pine's low density, he found it indispensable in the building of ships and their masts and spars. With characteristic ingenuity he created practical and attractive furniture that has been little improved upon in two hundred years.

At dinner his family sat on "jointed stools," ate with "treen ware" (wooden plates and spoons) at a wooden table. The master of the house sat in a chair, if he could afford one; he was the "chair man of the board." He respected wood for its versatility and acknowledged his dependence upon it by depicting trees on his coins and flags. The forest dominated and supported his life.

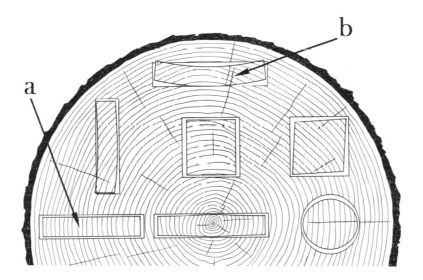

If one is willing to pay the price (in time as well as in dollars), one may be able to find old, clear pine boards. Many eighteenth- and ninteenth-century farmers placed such material in the attic for flooring and possible future use; ordinarily these were not fastened down. (An ad for these attic boards placed in a local newspaper or farm journal might bring interesting results.)

Today eastern white pine is sold in most lumberyards. It is available in many grades

7

A Word on Wood

from the highest quality — almost blemish-free material known as "select and better" — to a common grade that allows knots and other defects. Only the former grade is good enough for cabinetwork. When purchasing today's finished or planed lumber, you will find that a board referred to as a 1 x 5 was indeed rough-sawn to this size, but it has been machined down to a ¾ x 4½. Generally, the eighteenth-century "joyner" cut his logs with a pit saw into "all-purpose boards" somewhat thicker than 1 inch. On special boards for tabletops he removed the vertical saw marks with an adz. He handled this tool with amazing accuracy; with pendulum strokes he sliced off paper-thin shavings until a smooth surface was achieved.

If you can purchase your lumber in the rough, you may be able to get the yard or mill to plane 1-inch boards to ⅞ inch instead of the customary ¾ inch. After edge-gluing into wide panels the wood will be surfaced with a "smoothing" plane. The final thickness will be nearer to ¾ inch.

One can better understand the characteristic shrinkage and distortion of boards and other wooden shapes during the drying process by looking at the cross section of a tree, as shown on the previous page. The dimension changes shown are somewhat exaggerated.

The grain of a board is determined by the annular rings. As a tree grows, each year it forms a dense ring in the winter and a soft ring in summer. It is the count of these rings which reveals a tree's age. A board cut with these annular rings vertical to its large face, as shown at *a*, is said to be "quarter-sawn." One that is cut along the chord of an annular ring, as shown at *b*, is said to be "plain-sawn."

Boards at your lumberyard are usually available in widths up to 10 or 12 inches. Plain-sawn lumber in these widths may well have suffered checking in the cupped face where the planer squeezed the boards flat during the machine planing process. To detect these checks, pick up a board at the end and bend it slightly across the grain; the slightest pressure will expose them. These checks, while hardly visible in the planed board, will become accentuated when they are stained. Generally speaking, you will get the best stock for making panels from properly dried and planed clear boards ranging from 4 to 8 inches in width; the narrower boards are often less expensive than the wider ones and they are less likely to be spoiled by planer checks.

Artificially kiln-dried material is far more satisfactory for home workshop use than is air-dried stock, unless the latter has been dried over a period of many years. The kiln treat-

A Word on Wood

ment relieves many of the stresses set up in pine during drying and the lumber has much less tendency to expand and contract with seasonal changes in humidity than does wood of recent vintage dried naturally.

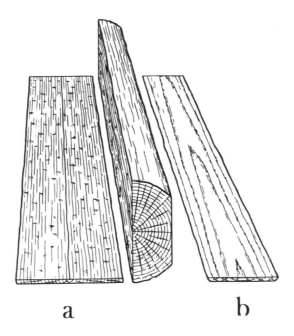

a   b

Techniques of seasoning lumber were well known to the colonists. Even as far back as the year A.D. 460, the Roman architect Vitruus recommended that freshly cut lumber be cured under water or in ox dung for a period of at least a month before air drying; this soaking or burial leeched out any sap that might have been in the wood.

Today, most "furniture" logs are cut during the winter when the sap is in the roots. The best technique is still to float the logs in a pond before air and kiln drying. In the spring, the floating logs are taken to the mill where they are cut into boards. These rough-sawn boards are carefully stacked in piles at a slight angle to the ground to improve drainage. Between each row of boards and running across the pile are placed a quantity of fungicide-treated sticks to assure good seasoning and ventilation. A flat roof of inferior boards is laid

A Word on Wood

on top of the pile to cut down on the impact of the sun's rays and to protect the lumber from rain; stones piled on the roof prevent the wind from dislodging it. After much of its moisture has been removed naturally, the lumber is taken to the kiln for final drying.

When purchasing lumber, make sure it is dry when you purchase it by asking your dealer to check it with his moisture meter. This is an electrical device, about the size of a pound of butter, with sharp prongs on the bottom which can be prodded into the wood. The current passing between the points is registered on a gauge that indicates the percentage of moisture in the wood fibers. The meter should read about 8 percent, certainly no higher than 10 percent. A higher reading indicates that the lumber has too much moisture for cabinet use. Lumber with a moisture content from 10 to 15 percent can be placed in the attic with "varnished" sticks between the boards until they have dried. Leave the attic door open so that the boards will have adequate ventilation.

Wood with a high moisture content will continue to shrink as it dries; if made into a piece of furniture and restrained from shrinking it would surely crack. Keep in mind that even properly dried wood will swell and shrink somewhat across the grain during changes in humidity (it will remain fairly constant in length).

To allow for this "come and go," cleats on the underside of a tabletop should be attached with roundheaded screws in oversize holes; washers under the screw heads will assist in this transverse movement. It is interesting to note that chairs and tables of the colonial period, which gave stalwart service to generations, suddenly deteriorate when thrown into the arid environment of the twentieth-century living room.

The pine you choose should be free of large areas of "blue stain," a fungus caused by improper drying. Blue-stained areas will have a tendency to appear much darker than the surrounding wood when you apply the oil-stain finish. Blue-stained wood may be used in the "stretchers," or undertable supports, in the bottoms and backs of blanket chests.

"Brown staining," on the other hand, is caused by improper kiln procedure. It is a surface discoloration, most of which will be planed off. Even if it is not removed in its entirety, it will blend well with the subsequent oil-stain finish.

There may be other species of pine available in your lumberyard that can substitute for eastern pine; of these Idaho is the closest in texture. However, red, ponderosa, southern yellow, and western sugar may be considered substitutes if the wood to be oil-stained is

A Word on Wood

first primed (see Finishing, pages 64–69). These latter woods, when finished naturally, do not have the broad, faint graining of pumpkin pine.

Another fine wood that is especially desirable in cabinetmaking (and is indigenous to New England) is hard or rock maple, as its name implies, a material that can be subjected to hard usage. Maple has always been the first choice of woodturners for table and chair legs. Few other woods are structurally superior for this use. Maple is far more dense than eastern white pine and so much more difficult for the amateur to work that only limited use is made of it in the designs here. Where a part is called for in maple, such as the leg of a table, the finial of a cradle, or a drawer knob, a supplier is listed under Sources, 12.

It may appear that I'm overstressing the use of eastern white pine in reproductions because it is easier to work and because it was the wood originally used by the early joyners. There is yet another reason. Its surface pores are extremely small and quite uniform in size, making it ideal for the application of an oil-base stain. It offers the best surface to the amateur who wants to achieve a finish something close to the natural patina of centuries-old wood. But we must do what we can to assure generations of the future that this wood of such marvelous attributes does not disappear from our forests.

From the days when the agents for the British navy marked the "king's pines" for His Majesty's frigates and merchantmen, the Maine woods have been an unending source of pulpwood and timber. These 17.7 million acres of forestland are greater in size than the combined areas of Vermont, New Hampshire, and Massachusetts. Unfortunately, about half of this acreage is owned by a handful of paper companies who view their timberlands as a pulpwood factory for their own mills. Mechanical harvesters, enormous machines that fell trees and strip their limbs, cut down every tree in their path. Today, the ubiquitous ax has been replaced by these more ravenous machines of destruction. At the mills, huge machines called "slashers" cut these timbers into four-foot lengths, convenient for conversion to pulp. Thus the noble white pine is being engulfed and ignominiously destined to become paper towels, tissue, or newsprint.

The paper industry spokesmen champion the causes of silviculture (the new term for modern, scientific woods management), saying that they look upon the forest as a renewable source. Yet the truth of the matter is that the largest of the pulp mills does not see fit to plant its stripped fields with "genetically improved seeds or seedlings," but leaves the

A Word on Wood

land prey to the erosion of rain and wind in hopes that nature will do their reforesting for them. There is great pressure on the part of absentee management to realize the greatest profit for the least amount of work, and owners feel they cannot afford to treat the forests as a long-term investment.*

Fortunately, there are some lumber mills in Maine and New Hampshire that treat the majestic white pine with the care it deserves, and from these holdings, for a while at least, Americans will be able to get a high quality of pumpkin pine for home workshop use.

* William C. Osborn, *The Paper Plantation*, New York: Grossman Publishers, 1974.

Tools of the Trade

How OFTEN have you looked at an antique table or cradle, standing in its rightful historical setting, admired its clean lines and the warm patina of its aged wood, and then marveled that it could have been fashioned with the "crude" tools of centuries past. Certainly the man who made it was a rare individual, an artist and genius of sorts.

This book is keyed to the person who, with little or no woodworking experience, would like to reproduce some of this furniture using only the absolutely essential tools. Anyone with such a desire should not let the glamorous advertisements showing "totally equipped" and costly home workshops dampen his aspiration. With some ingenuity and a few functional tools one can readily compensate for the lack of expensive equipment. Power tools may expedite the construction process, but one can easily miss the greatest reward of all, the real enjoyment of hand tool skills and an understanding of primitive construction.

I shall try to guide you to the kinds of high-grade hand tools that were used in the old days and will direct you to suppliers who take pride in supplying items such as beechwood and hornbeam hand planes, made in Germany today as they have been for centuries. Sources of lathe turnings in maple are noted since such turnings are an integral part of several designs and are difficult for the beginner to make.

As a single concession to the modern age, one power tool is recommended as essential to the woodworking operations explained here: a circular table saw powered by an electric motor. With this and simple hand tools, a novice can build a variety of treasures which he can proudly display.

For best general use, a table saw should have a ribbed, cast-iron table whose surface, of good size, has been accurately planed and grooved (for guiding a cutoff miter gauge). It should be equipped with rigid, well-graduated guides front and back for securing the "fence," or guide used in ripping (making lengthwise cuts).

The saw arbor, with its shaft (usually $\frac{5}{8}$ inch in diameter) on which the saw blade is clamped between flanges, should be securely mounted on a framework which moves in trunions, or bearings, so that it may be tilted with relation to the table surface, thereby permitting bevel cuts along the edges of boards. The mounting of the motor and saw should also be capable of being raised and lowered with relation to the surface of the table to provide cuts of various depths. The motor should be $\frac{3}{4}$ or preferably 1 horsepower, single phase, and 110 volts. It is desirable to choose a sawtable that will accept a 10-inch saw blade, although for most work you may prefer to use an 8-inch blade.

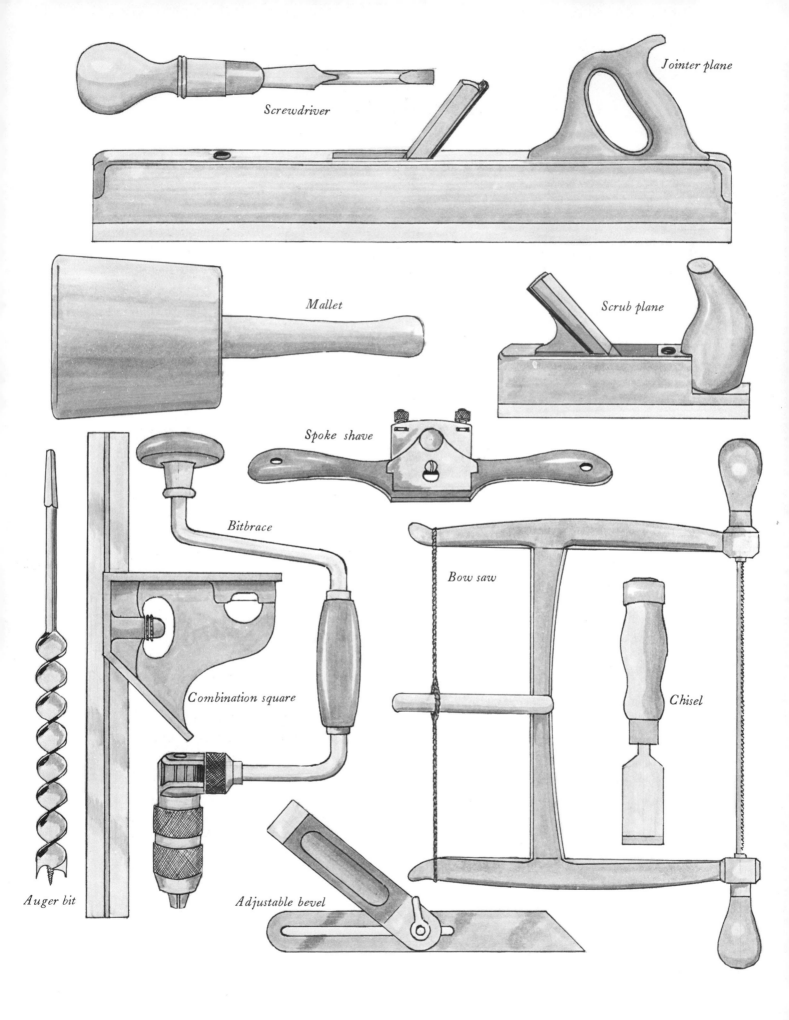

Screwdriver

Jointer plane

Mallet

Scrub plane

Spoke shave

Bitbrace

Bow saw

Combination square

Chisel

Auger bit

Adjustable bevel

Tools of the Trade

The saw should come equipped with a miter gauge, that is, a quadrant mounted on a steel bar that slides in the grooves of the sawtable, serving as a "pusher" and guide when cutting boards across the grain. The quadrant can readily be adjusted to make angular cuts. For cutting small, narrow pieces of wood, always use a "pusher stick" (see Ripping and Rabbeting, pages 35–36). Never fail to use this stick when the fingers would otherwise get close to the rotating blade. Only the foolhardy will fail to have such a stick hanging within easy reach.

Above the table and the saw blade there should be a guard, usually hinged to a thin piece of steel called a "splitter," which keeps the cut stock from pinching in on the saw blade, as it sometimes tends to do. Use the sawguard whenever possible.

The sawtable should have an insert with a slot through which the blade can be raised and lowered. These inserts are usually made of aluminum or plywood and can be replaced when worn.

The control switch of the motor should be within convenient reach of the operator and should be able to be locked or totally disconnected when not in use, lest it serve as an overwhelming temptation for children.

An accessory called a molding head, which can be mounted in place of the saw blade, will enable you to cut various molding shapes (similar to picture molding) along the edges of boards.

The saw blade for best general use is an 8- or 10-inch combination circular saw. This is easily and economically sharpened and if properly maintained will leave a ripped edge suitable for gluing. Do not use a saw that is dull. Prolonged use may overheat the blade, possibly resulting in warping and permanent damage. If you cannot sharpen the saw yourself, find someone who can by looking in the Yellow Pages under "Saws — Sharpening." Although the combination circular saw can be used for crosscutting, it cannot compare with the fine-toothed crosscut blades specifically designed for such use. Planer or hollow-ground saws are a delight to use, but they are a little more expensive and more difficult to sharpen. Carbide-tipped blades come under the same heading. The most common saws for home workshop use have a ⅝-inch-diameter shaft hole. It is quite easy, however, to have a professional saw shop enlarge the hole or insert a bushing to make it smaller if necessary. The saw when positioned on the shaft should have a "slide" fit and the teeth should point toward the operator. The nut on the shaft should hold the flange securely against the blade so that

Tools of the Trade

as it is rotated by hand it will be parallel to the face of the fence. If the saw blade wobbles as it turns, either the blade itself or the shaft on which it is mounted is bent and out of alignment and it is a poor investment.

The twentieth century has produced another type of power saw called a radial saw, in which the motor and the saw are suspended from an overhead track above the wood to be worked. Crosscutting is done by moving the motor and the saw across the board. Ripping is done with the motor and the saw clamped in one position. These radial saws are generally more expensive and less accurate than the standard table saw and are, in my opinion, more dangerous for amateur use.

More often than not, a secondhand table saw is every bit as good as a new one. Manufacturers of woodworking equipment have not yet succumbed to the credo of planned obsolescence. A search for a table saw in the classified ads of your newspaper may be especially rewarding. The auction page of the Sunday paper may reveal a "garage" sale of shop equipment that includes just what you want. A small classified ad saying "Table Saw Wanted" or "Will swap family heirloom [player piano, grandmother's doll carriage, sheet music of the twenties] for Woodworking Tools" may bring in some good leads. It may even uncover a supply of well-dried pumpkin pine as a by-product. The Yellow Pages of the telephone directory often list woodworking equipment dealers who are usually anxious to sell machines taken as trade-ins on new equipment. If you locate a used table saw that seems to fill your needs, check it over thoroughly for possible hidden flaws or damage. Check the shaft, or arbor, for alignment and wear. If you can force the shaft up by lifting the protruding end while the table remains flat, the bearings are worn. Worn ball bearings can be replaced at very little expense, but a worn babbit or lead bearing may indicate an expensive repair. Other sources of table saws and their accessories are listed in the back of the book in Section 3.

Now a word about hand tools. Superior hand tools of steel and wood have largely disappeared from the American scene. They have been almost eclipsed by modern mass-production techniques. Fortunately, much of the furniture industry in England, Germany, and Switzerland is far less mechanized than ours, and a demand still exists for quality tools, such as smoothing planes made from a block of beechwood with a hornbeam shoe, wood-frame bow saws, and beautifully tempered steel chisels. Succeeding generations of

Tools of the Trade

craftsmen in Sheffield, England, have taken great pride in their work so that the stamp on a chisel or plane blade "Warranted cast steel, Sheffield" was and still is a mark of the highest quality.

A search for eighteenth-century hand tools in secondhand or antique shops may uncover a cache of planes and chisels finer than any made today. If you are lucky enough to find some of these antique molding planes, they will be practical to use and attractive to display.

Remember, it pays to buy good quality, even if the price seems high. See Sources 1, 2, for names of manufacturers and dealers selling these tools.

Some of the hand tools to look for are:

> Set of screwdrivers — small, medium and large
> Set of chisels — $\frac{1}{8}$", $\frac{1}{4}$", $\frac{3}{8}$", $\frac{1}{2}$", $\frac{3}{4}$"
> Set of drills $\frac{1}{16}$" to $\frac{1}{4}$" by 64ths
> Set of auger bits $\frac{1}{4}$", $\frac{5}{16}$", $\frac{3}{8}$", $\frac{1}{2}$", $\frac{5}{8}$", $\frac{3}{4}$", 1", and $1\frac{1}{4}$"
> Combination square
> Scribing dividers
> Pencil compass
> Hammer
> Center punch
> Jackknife
> Mallet
> Combination oilstone
> Tape measure
> Block plane
> Scrub plane
> Jointer plane
> Bow saw
> Steel spoke shave
> Four-in-hand file, or shoe rasp
> Bitbrace
> Hand drill
> Clamps

Tools of the Trade

Handsaws needed:

26″ crosscut — 8 point
26″ rip — 5 point
12″ back — 15 point

A Workbench

Your workbench will participate in more hours of work with you than any other part of your equipment, so you should give it careful thought and workmanship.

Ideally, a workbench should be of extra-heavy construction, strongly cross-braced and securely lag-screwed to a very solid wall.

Because many craftsmen live in rented quarters with rigid restrictions regarding wall fastening and because modern business life may involve frequent moves, this ideal bench setup remains an impossible dream.

The following directions will produce a very good compromise with these limitations and provide a good, solid worktable that will be free-standing and can be easily dismounted for moving if necessary.

A most satisfactory workbench can be made by fastening a *solid-core* 30-inch wide door panel of any convenient length (preferably hardwood faced) on top of two carpenter's horses. Sawhorse brackets for making such a bench are available at most lumberyards or may be purchased from dealers listed in Sources, 1.

The horses can be easily made using Douglas fir 2 x 4's and 1 x 4 stock. Cut four legs for each horse approximately 36 inches long, using good straight 2 x 4's. These legs should be attached to a 2 x 4 crossbar with sawhorse brackets, as shown. The crossbar should be approximately 26 inches long, or 4 inches shorter than the bench width.

Be sure that the 2 x 4 legs are snugly fitted into the clamps and that the wing nuts on the clamps are tightly turned so that the clamps securely grip the crossbar. With the legs securely clamped, cut and fit cleats or crossbracing to the legs as shown, with the top edges of the cleats about 8 inches above floor level. The long cleats can be glued and nailed to each pair of legs, but the short cleats should be screwed in place without glue so that the legs may be dismounted. When the cleats have been attached, stand the horse on a level surface and, with dividers, scribe the foot of each leg for cutting to give a bench height of 33 to 36 inches, depending upon your own height.

Make a shelf for each horse as shown, using ¾-inch plywood. These shelves will hold cement blocks or other ballast to give the bench weight and stability. If the blocks do not give sufficient weight, fill the hollows in the blocks with cement and stone.

Glue and screw-fasten a 4 x 4 clamp timber (you may glue and clamp together two 2 x 4 pieces if necessary), which should be straight and square, beneath the front edge of the benchtop, as shown at *a*. Douglas fir is the best material.

A Workbench

Position the top assembly on the horses with the crossbars of the horses against the clamp timber. The bars should be perpendicular to the front edge and in from the ends of the panel by about 18 inches. The benchtop should be fastened to the horses with ⅜ x 6 flathead stove bolts, as shown at *b*. The heads of the stove bolts should be countersunk and there

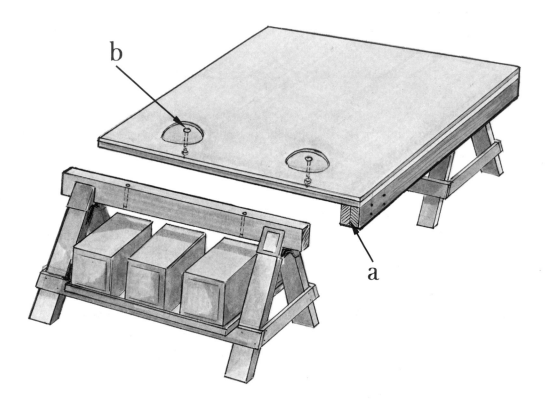

should be washers under the nuts. A cover board of ¼-inch plywood or Masonite of the same size as the panel should be screw-fastened to it to protect it from damage during work. It should not be glued down, since it may need to be replaced from time to time.

Slide bar clamps, for example, ones having a 4-inch depth and a 10-inch bar, may be used to hold work in place on the benchtop and are also very flexible for general use (see Sources, 1).

A Workbench

A bench vise may be mounted near the left front corner of the benchtop as indicated in the drawing. A good woodworker's vise of ample size is moderately expensive, but will be found to be very useful and a good timesaver. I recommend that you not skimp on the size or the price if you decide to install one (see Sources, 1).

Tools and Where to Put Them

Some orderly mind, perhaps a skilled Shaker craftsman, gave us the adage, "A place for everything and everything in its place." Certainly the most attractive workshop is the one in which tools are hung resplendently on the walls. Full-color pictures in various magazines present seductive and often tantalizing displays of such perfection.

But what can the craftsman do when he is renting an apartment or home where restrictions prevent the wall-fastening of perforated board for tool display? It is sensible to think in terms of something other than the conventional system for storing tools and accessories.

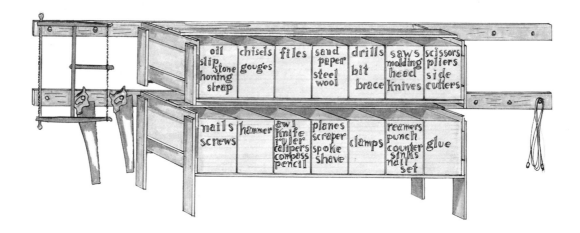

An obviously simple system is one in which tools are placed in labeled boxes or drawers on shelves. The shelving can be made of low-grade lumber and the boxes standard gallon-size 200-pound-test corrugated cartons (see Sources, 11.) These cartons come flat and are easily made into usable storage boxes by gluing the ends shut (a clamp will hold glued surfaces until dry) and by cutting open one of the sides as shown — forming in effect a sturdy drawer that can be slid on and off the shelves at will. Measure the corrugated carton you plan to use and decide how many cartons per section will be suitable for the space available. Make a base, or frame, from 1 x 4 lumber to fit the multiple of the carton size as shown in the drawing. At each of the four corners of the frame, glue and screw (or nail) 1 x 4 uprights of a proper length so that there will be a 1-inch clearance above the top of the cartons (drawers) after the sections are stacked. To support succeeding sections, fasten

Tools and Where to Put Them

1 x 3 cleats across the uprights as shown. Floor over the bottom frame with ¼-inch plywood.

Extensions to hold longer or larger tools should be screw-fastened to the backs of the shelving. Shaker pegs (see Sources, 12) inserted in these will hold the tools. These extensions can be readily removed if necessary.

The lower set of shelves should be supported by legs, as shown, to make floor cleaning easier.

The top shelf should be covered with a panel of ¼-inch plywood or cardboard to keep dust from settling in the boxes.

These self-supporting shelves can hold a saw, a long fence, and other fixtures on nails or pegs driven into the ends of the sections.

This type of organization is used industrially and it will make sense in your workshop. The cardboard boxes are big enough to hold a bitbrace together with your drills and bits. Small drills may be kept in a glass screw-top jar and the longer ones in a metal coffee can, or a few holes of compatible size bored into a block of wood will make an inexpensive stand that can be marked to indicate drill sizes.

The advantage of this system is that most of your tools can be stored together with their related accessories, as shown. Your own imagination and versatility can supply many combinations. You will notice the convenience of this type of storage when you have a job to do at a distance from your shop and you want to take along specific tools and their components.

Joints and Joinery

MANY WOODWORKING TECHNIQUES have remained the same for thousands of years, beginning with the days when the Egyptians built their river boats of Lebanese cedar using an adz, saws, and chisels of hardened bronze.

Gradually there evolved a method of repeatedly heating and hammering an alloy of iron and carbon to produce wrought-iron tools that would "hold and edge," which the colonial American joyner used so effectively. It remained for the English to make a real breakthrough in this slow, arduous, and uncertain process when they produced a crucible, or "cast steel," just prior to the American Revolution. As a result of this metallurgical advancement, saws, chisels, and other tools of superior quality were developed.

With sharp tools and with accuracy in their use, the joints shown here are easy to make. All of these methods of joinery were commonly known to the seventeenth-century cabinetmaker. They are still favored in the twentieth century.

One of the simplest methods of putting two boards together at right angles is the butt joint (the boards are "abutting" one another), of which there are almost endless variations, see *a* to *e*. One of the most desirable is the double lap joint, which has been in use for centuries. The shoulders of this joint hold boards in accurate alignment while the nails or pegs, together with glue, make a secure construction. Since the shoulders are blind, or hidden, the joints have been popular in making drawer fronts, where it is undesirable to have the end grain of the side pieces exposed. While the pegs originally used were often slightly tapered, and sometimes square in cross section, their modern counterparts (about 1/4 inch in diameter) have multiple grooves running with the axis (see Sources, 12). These grooves have been compressed into the peg and by expanding, when glued, contribute to making exceedingly tight joints.

One of the most secure of all joints is the mortise and tenon (f_1, f_2, f_3). It is a construction that has lasted for centuries and can be seen in the furniture of ancient Greece. Because of its strength, it was favored by early American craftsmen. It was often employed in making the base of a table or in similar framework construction. It consists of a *tenon* that is cut on the end of a piece of stock called a *rail* so that it may be inserted into a *mortise*, or hole, cut into a piece called a *post*. The tenon is readily made on the circular saw (see End Sawing, page 41, *a*). Unless one has specialized power tools, the mortise is most often made by hand.

The tenon is made by cutting away from each side of a rail sufficient stock to leave two

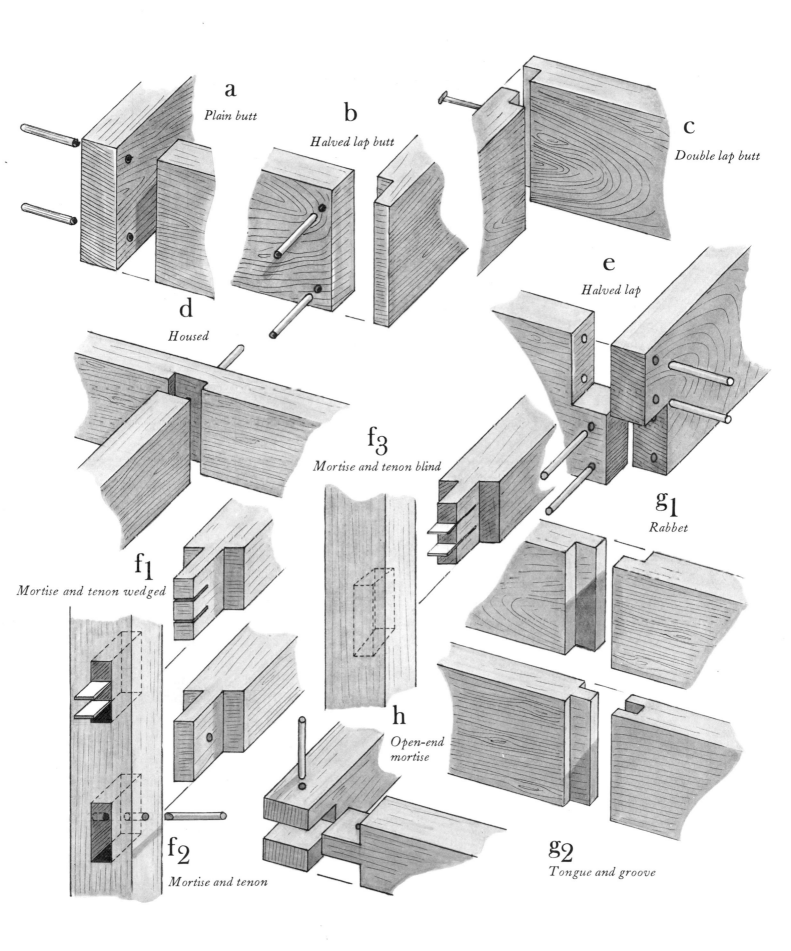

a
Plain butt

b
Halved lap butt

c
Double lap butt

d
Housed

e
Halved lap

f₃
Mortise and tenon blind

f₁
Mortise and tenon wedged

f₂
Mortise and tenon

g₁
Rabbet

g₂
Tongue and groove

h
Open-end mortise

Joints and Joinery

shoulders. A common practice is to divide the end area into thirds, cutting away two thirds to leave the remaining center third as a tenon. It is very important that each shoulder be exactly the same distance from the end of the rail. The tenon should be long enough to go completely through the post (unless it is a "blind" tenon like f_3). In some cases it may be undesirable for the end grain to show and a blind tenon can be made with the length of the tenon somewhat less than the thickness of the post. To cover the four edges of a mortise hole, it is sometimes desirable to make a "four-shouldered" tenon. This is accomplished by reducing the width of the tenon by a small and equal amount on each side (see End Sawing, page 41, e).

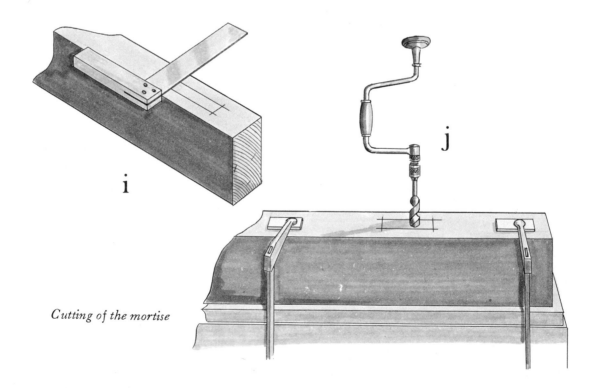

Cutting of the mortise

The mortise should be made so that the tenon fits it accurately; any looseness will result in a weak joint. With a sharp pencil and a square, mark the outline of the mortise on the

Joints and Joinery

post; this should be the exact cross section of the tenon, as shown at *i*. Repeat this marking on the opposite face so that you may check frequently to be sure the walls of the finished

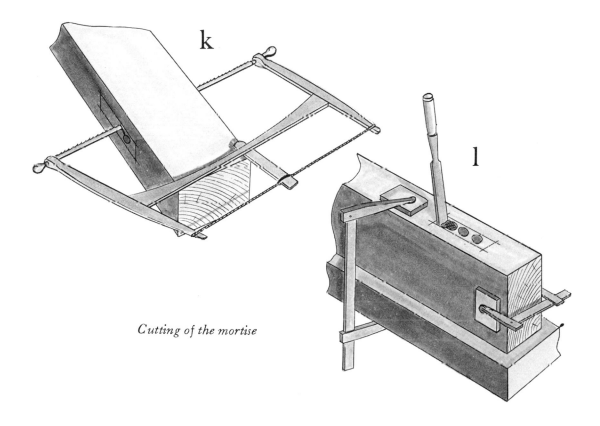

Cutting of the mortise

mortise will be square and parallel to the outside faces of the post. To prevent damage to the workbench surface while making the mortise, clamp the post on a "backup" board and to the workbench. The post should be clamped on its side conveniently near the edge of the workbench. If the mortise is to be made near the end of a post, it should be cross-clamped as shown at *l* to prevent possible splitting. With a brace and bit held in a vertical position, drill one or more holes well within the marked rectangle, as shown at *j*. If a blind mortise is being made, drill only slightly deeper than the length of the tenon.

Joints and Joinery

The through mortise may be "rough-cleaned" of waste material by using a bow saw, as shown at k. To use the saw in this manner, remove the blade from the frame, insert the blade in the previously drilled hole, and reinsert the blade in the saw frame. Remove the waste wood in the mortise by sawing within $\frac{1}{16}$ inch of the lines, but no closer. The remainder of the wood should be removed with a sharp chisel, a four-in-hand file, or a shoe rasp (see Sources, 1). A piece of sandpaper wrapped about the file may be used to achieve the final smooth finish. When making a blind mortise, smaller and more numerous holes may be necessary than when making a through mortise, the wood waste being removed to the required depth using a chisel, as shown at l.

When ready to assemble the joint, apply glue to the walls of the mortise and to the faces of the tenon. When the joint is properly assembled the shoulders should be tight against the post and the rail should be perpendicular to the post. When the glue is set, drill a $\frac{1}{4}$-inch hole (centered in the joint) three-quarters of the way through the post. Apply glue to the hole and pin and drive in the pin. Cut the pin flush with the post surface and sand until the surface is smooth.

When mortise and tenon joints were used in barn and house framing, the hole in the tenon was made slightly closer to the shoulders than it would have been if drilled as suggested, see f_2. As the "treenail" (pronounced *trunnel*), or wedge-pointed peg, was driven, it pulled the shoulders against the post. Sometimes the post was made of freshly cut wood, while the tenoned rail was made from well-dried stock. As the post dried, it shrunk about the tenon, making a secure joint.

Tenons, particularly blind tenons, were often held securely by means of a wedge or wedges driven into saw cuts in the end of the tenon, as shown in f_3. You will notice in the sketches that the mortises used in this construction are slightly wider at the interior end than at the surface opening to allow for expansion of the tenon as the wedges are driven into place.

There are many other joinery designs of which you may be aware, such as the dovetails used in Egyptian sarcophagi five thousand years ago, but these were less commonly found in simple furniture and they are somewhat more difficult for the amateur to execute.

Safeguards and Sawguards

Your power saw is a cooperative and productive working partner, but it is also a jealous one. It demands respect, attention, and a slow pace, and it will strike back if these attributes are denied. Here are a few safeguards that will demonstrate your good faith:

1. *Never* use the saw when you are in a hurry. If you do not have ample time, postpone your work.
2. *Never* use the saw when small children are in the vicinity.
3. *Never* use the saw if you are wearing a loose necktie or scarf, flapping, unbuttoned sleeves, or long hair that is untied.
4. *Never* attempt to put work through the saw in a reverse direction.
5. *Never* use the fence (alone) as a stop when crosscutting to make cuts of uniform length. The free piece may wedge between the blade and the fence and kick back.
6. *Never* force the work against the will of the saw. If it binds, smokes, chatters, or otherwise resists — *stop*. Find what is wrong and correct it.

Minimize your risk of accident: Make sure that the guard is in place over the saw blade whenever possible.

Be doubly on guard when the size or shape of the work piece is unusually large or small.

Small sizes are always difficult to work and require *extra care* and special guides and/or push sticks to keep hands and fingers away from the saw-blade area.

When using extra long or wide stock, note the directions given in Ripping and Rabbeting, pages 35–36.

Sawguards come as standard equipment on most table saws made today. If your table saw does not have one, you can purchase it as a separate unit (see Sources, 4). The metal and plastic guard shown in the sketches is the most common type. It is mounted on the table with a vertical metal plate directly behind the saw blade. This plate acts as a splitter and holds the saw cut, or kerf, apart so as to prevent the wood from binding against the saw.

If you have a heavy-duty or industrial type of table saw, the guard that would be best suited to it would be the 34-885 Uniguard sold by Rockwell. This guard can be adapted to fit most any table and can be folded aside when not in use.

Jointing an Edge by Machine

THE TERM "jointing" refers to the process of machining the edge of a board so that it is relatively straight along its entire length and so that the edge thus created is perpendicular to the board's flat faces. This is the process used to prepare boards for subsequent gluing, one to another, to form a panel. This is one joint that the home craftsman finds most difficult to make using a hand plane. If it is not made accurately, the glue joint will be conspicuous and of little value structurally. It is, on the other hand, a relatively easy joint to make on the circular saw, if a device called a long fence (*a*) is made and used as explained below. The woodworking industry has developed machines called "jointers" for machining the edge of a board, but the home craftsman of limited means and shop space need not invest in one.

To make a long fence, find a well-dried piece of hardwood, hard pine, fir or spruce 2 x 4 or larger in cross section and twice the length of the longest board you will be joining. If you plan to joint boards over 4 feet long, a long fence made from a 4 x 4 would be advisable. It should be free of twist and without knots that might affect it structurally. I suggest that you find old wood, if you can, since age imparts dimensional stability. If one edge of the board you have chosen for the long fence is not accurately flat and straight, take it to your lumberyard and ask them to joint the 4-inch face. It then might be well to ask the yard to rip the opposite face while holding the edge previously jointed against their saw fence, taking off as little stock as possible. The remaining two edges of the stock are not critical to the jointing operation and, unless they are considerably bowed, it is not necessary to have them accurately cut.

Sand your long fence lightly; give it a coat of sealer, varnish, or both to help preserve its straightness. It is not a bad idea to insert a stout screw eye in one end so that it can be hung vertically when not in use. Using number 12 steel wood screws, fasten the jointed (or opposite) face to the metal fence of the table saw with the ends of the long fence equidistant from the saw blade.

Assuming that one of the edges of your board to be jointed has a curved edge, as shown (*b*), position the board so that it touches the fence near its ends. If neither edge of the board can be positioned, remove any interfering high spots with a hand plane. This does not have to be done with any great accuracy.

Invariably, long boards will be difficult for one person to handle. Get the help of a friend or make a table support (*c*) to hold the stock while it is going through the saw.

Jointing an Edge by Machine

Using a carpenter's square, make certain that the saw blade is perpendicular to the surface of the sawtable. Raise the saw so that the teeth will just break through the wood when being sawed. Set the fence at a distance from the saw that will give you the longest jointed edge possible with the least saw waste. Be sure to keep the board tight against the fence during the entire cutting operation. Make sure that the guard is in position over the saw as shown.

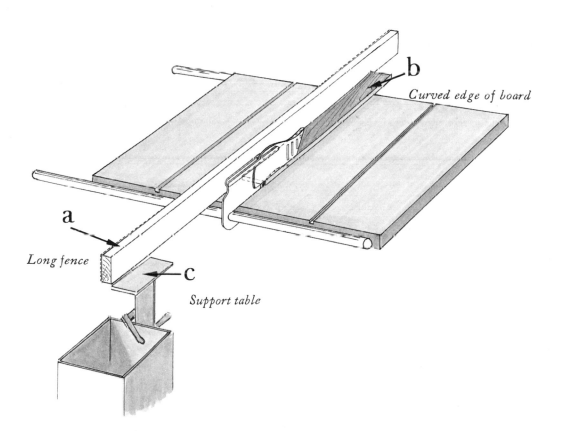

b

Curved edge of board

a

Long fence

c

Support table

Once the edge has been jointed, it is a simple matter to turn the board around, reset the fence as necessary and rip a parallel edge. The board is now ready for gluing on either of the edges.

If your long fence has a slight bow, as shown by the dotted lines, you will make a jointed

Jointing an Edge by Machine

edge that is slightly "hollow." This is the ideal edge for gluing, since the edges to be glued will touch at the ends and not in the center; the hollow will vanish when the board is clamped for gluing. The hollow, however, should not be in excess of $\frac{1}{16}$ inch per foot of joint to be glued. With this built-in "spring," there is little chance that the joint will ever open. See detail in Glues and Gluing, page 45.

Jointing an Edge by Hand

I F ONE DOES NOT HAVE a table saw on which to joint the edge of a board, the operation can be done with a jointer plane. The great length of this plane (*a*), usually about 24 inches, makes it ideally suited for preparing glue joints. The cutting edge of the blade, which should always be set to cut a fine shaving, can be adjusted or removed by hitting

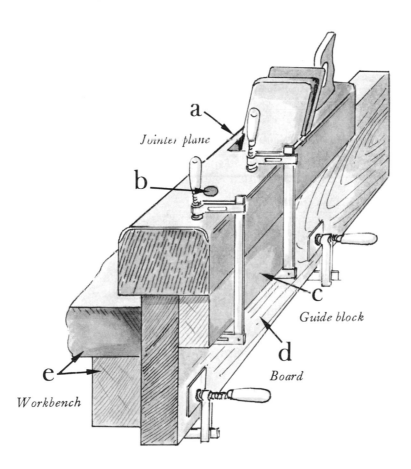

Jointer plane

Guide block

Board

Workbench

the striker knob (*b*) with a hammer. This knob is on the forward upper surface of the plane; when it is struck sharply, the vibration loosens the wedge that holds the blade in position. When aligning the blade, make sure that the straight cutting edge is parallel to

33

Jointing an Edge by Hand

the bottom, or sole, of the plane. The blade should be honed sharp before and while using.

The jointer plane spans the hollows along the edge to be straightened and it levels the high spots. To make sure that the finished edge is square with the side of the board to be jointed, clamp a guide block (*c*) to the forward body of the plane as shown. The block can be made about 1 inch wide, 1½ inches deep, and about 6 inches long, but not so long that it interferes with the cutting edge of the blade. The outer surface of the block should be even with the side of the plane. The block should be made of maple or another hardwood; it should be made straight and square. While planing, a right-handed person would grip the handle with the right hand while the left holds the guide block tightly against the board (*d*). Because of the nature of wood, some pieces can be planed better in one direction than another. To facilitate planing, rub the sole and the inner face of the guide block with a piece of candle or wax.

When finished with the plane, store it on its side or, better still, loosen the wedge and position the blade within the plane so that the cutting edge will not be damaged.

Ripping and Rabbeting

RIPPING REFERS to the process of cutting a board lengthwise so as to produce a piece of narrower width. In doing this, the previously jointed edge of the board is held tightly against the fence while the flat face of the stock rests on the tabletop. It is not advisable to attempt to rip stock that has not been previously jointed, because the edge may be crooked. As a result, the board may become jammed between the saw and the fence or kicked back toward the operator.

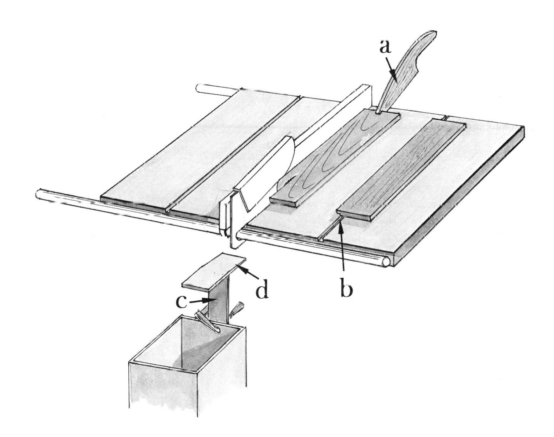

Use a special ripping saw or a combination saw mounted with the teeth pointing toward the operator. For safety, set the saw blade so that it just breaks through the wood as the cut

Ripping and Rabbeting

progresses. When cutting, use one hand to keep the board against the fence, and one to push the board forward against the saw, but *keep both hands away from the saw area*. For small pieces, use a push-stick (*a* on previous page) to assist the stock through the saw. Make sure that the saw-guard is in place.

If, after the cut has been made, the free wood between the saw blade and the fence does not clear itself and fall to the floor, do *not* try to remove it with your hands while the motor is still running.

To make a rabbet, cut a rectangular notch along the edge of a piece of previously jointed stock, as shown at *b*. The rabbet is generally made in two operations, with separate saw and fence settings for each cut. After adjusting the fence to the proper position, make the first cut with the stock standing on edge. Readjust the fence and make the second cut with the stock lying flat on the sawtable. It should be noted that the "free piece," or waste remaining after the second cut, may be ejected forcefully by the saw, so the operator should stand to one side at the finish of the cut.

An extra pair of hands is the best help when stock being cut is extra long or wide. When a helper is not available, a support stand can be used and will supply some assistance. The simplest of these support stands is shown and consists essentially of a small wooden box, weighted so as to be steady and stable, to which various types of supports may be clamped and adjusted.

When making a support stand to assist you in ripping extra long stock, clamp a vertical board (*c*) to the weighted box. A top board (*d*), which has been planed to a wedge on the edge nearest to the table saw, is nailed at its center to the vertical board as shown. The upper face of the top board should be at table height; adjust the vertical board to make this alignment.

Resawing

RESAWING, the operation of reducing the thickness of a board or plank by sawing it into two or more thinner boards, is performed as a ripping operation. The saw blade should be raised to half the width of the plank to be cut. This requires a sharp saw. If the blade will not reach the halfway mark, it should be raised as high as possible. The stock should be held firmly against the fence by a spring, as shown at *a*.

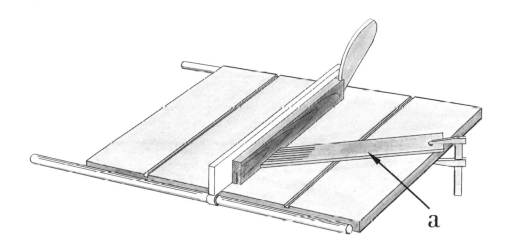

a

The spring is made from a piece of ¾-by-4-inch hardwood, such as maple, cut long enough so that it can be conveniently clamped to the tabletop. Into one end of the wood a series of parallel cuts is made, spaced about ⅜ inch apart, with the table saw. The length of these cuts should be 3 or 4 inches, or great enough to give the wood spring effect. The end of the spring in which the cuts are made should be cut at a 45-degree angle so that the plank being cut will ride easily by it under pressure.

When the stock has been run through the saw, it should be turned in the other direction and, with the same face against the fence, run through the saw again. If the two saw cuts do not meet and separate the plank, clear out the intervening wood with a hand saw. It will help to clamp the plank to the bench during this operation.

It is not necessary to use the sawguard during resawing because the saw is entirely within the wood during most of the cutting.

Crosscutting

SQUARE CROSSCUTTING is making a right angle cut across a board which has been previously jointed on one edge. The jointed edge is placed against the miter gauge and both are moved toward the saw. The gauge moves in a groove which has been machined into the top of the sawtable. This groove should be parallel to the fence, and it can be used to check the accuracy of the fence adjustment. A sawtable invariably has two of these grooves, but most cutting is done with the gauge in the groove to the left of the saw. For greater accuracy in cutting long boards, an auxiliary wood facing (*a*), about 24 inches in length, may be centered on the miter gauge and screwed to it. This auxiliary face is usually

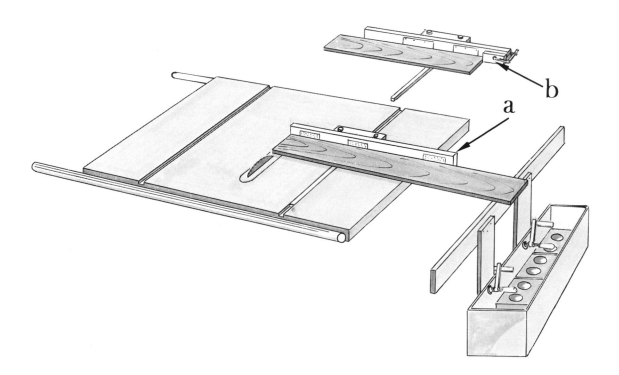

made from a 1 x 3 whose faces have been made straight and parallel. As an added help, tack two or three pieces of sandpaper to the auxiliary face to prevent the work from sliding once it has been positioned for cutting. A stop (*b*) may be clamped to the auxiliary face to facilitate holding.

Crosscutting

Short pieces of wood, 6 inches or less in length, are difficult and dangerous to handle on a power saw and are much better worked with a hand saw.

Boards which extend over 3 feet beyond the table surface should be held up by a crosscut support, as shown. This is simply a frame the length of the sawtable. The frame is attached to a weighted base and can be adjusted in height using clamps. The top edge of the rest is the same height as the tabletop.

The sawguard is usually removed during crosscutting because it interferes with the movement of the miter gauge and its auxiliary face. Both hands should support the stock to the left of the saw as the wood is being cut. Never support or push the free piece to the right of the saw. Do not attempt to remove the waste or free material by flicking it away with a stick or fingers while the saw is moving; shut off the machine before clearing the waste.

Miter Crosscutting

ITER CROSSCUTTING is somewhat more difficult than square crosscutting because the stock has a tendency to "crawl" while the work is passing through the saw, thus making an inaccurate miter joint. A stop may be clamped to the auxiliary face as shown at *a*. Sandpaper tacked on the face will help to prevent the stock from creeping. It is also possible to drive some brads into the auxiliary face, then filing the exposed brads to sharp points; these barbs should project just above the surface of the wood.

During the entire cut hold the stock firmly against the auxiliary face.

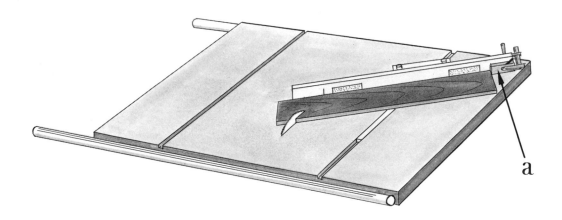

a

End Sawing

To cut an open mortise in the end of stock, and to do it with accuracy and safety, make an "end cutting fixture" as shown. This device is made from a "base block" of wood approximately 2 x 4 x 18 inches, jointed and ripped, marked *a*, to which is glued a "vertical support" (*b*) of ½-inch plywood or planed wood approximately 10

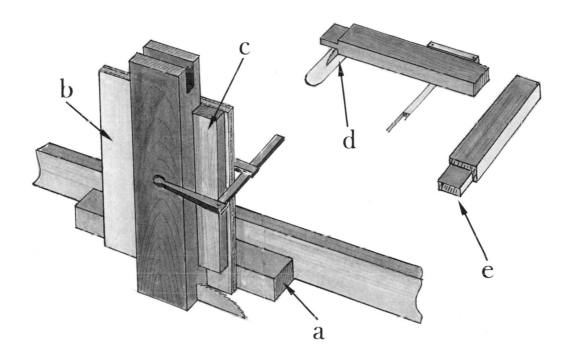

inches square. A "guide block" (*c*) about ¾ inch thick, 3 inches wide, and 6 inches long and with straight, parallel edges should be nailed and glued to *b* in a true vertical position; this will act as a guide and brace to hold the stock being cut in a perpendicular position. Use a clamp to hold the stock being cut as shown. Make successive cuts, adjusting the fence as necessary, until the desired width is achieved. The clamp handle makes a good rest for the right or steadying hand while the left holds the fixture tight against the fence while sawing.

The tenon of a joint can best be made on the circular saw, as shown at *d* and *e*, using both the end cutting fixture and the miter gauge.

Molding

MOLDING refers to the process of cutting grooves into the face or edge of a board. It is done on your power saw by means of a molding or cutter head that is mounted on the saw shaft in place of the saw blade. This molding head (*a*) holds specially shaped knives (*b*) at three equidistant points on its circumference. Knives may be used in combination to achieve a wide variety of molding designs (see Sources, 3). For clean cuts, make sure that the knives are properly sharpened. Make doubly sure that the knives are securely in place in the molding head before using.

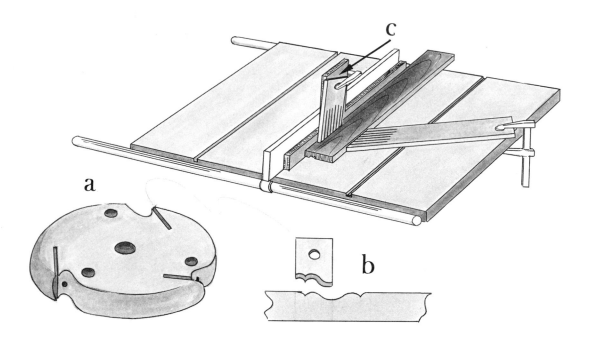

Since there are only three cutting edges in the molding head as compared with many teeth in a saw blade, it has a greater tendency to vibrate and it is more than ordinarily necessary that the work piece be held securely in two directions: horizontally against the fence and vertically against the surface of the sawtable. This is accomplished by making two "spring" boards (see Resawing, page 37), one to hold the work down, the other to hold it against the fence.

Molding

To support the vertical spring cut a piece of ¾-inch plywood into a T shape (*c*). This support should be clamped or screwed to the fence with the stem pointing upward as shown. The vertical spring is then clamped to the stem so that the bearing of the spring is centered over the cutter.

The horizontal spring should be clamped to the tabletop so that it will hold the stock firmly against the fence, which is faced with the vertical spring support.

If the moldings being cut require the removal of substantial quantities of wood, it may be desirable to accomplish this by means of several passes of the work over the rotating cutter head, raising the head by suitable amounts for each pass.

After using, remove the knives from the cutter head. Clean the knives and the head, removing all traces of pitch; wipe the blades with a little oil to keep them from rusting in storage. Store the knives so that the edges will not be nicked. It is not considered good practice to store the head with the blades inserted.

Glues and Gluing

For hundreds of years animal glue was the most common adhesive. This was made from the parings of hides, the ears of oxen and sheep, and the skins of other animals. This unpalatable mix is still available and, in spite of its drawbacks, is quite popular throughout the world. It comes in flake form and, in combination with a little water, must be heated in a double-boiler-type of glue pot whenever it is used. Early cabinetmakers used many glued blocks to secure and reinforce the joints in their cabinets. A block was coated with hot glue and "rubbed" into a secure position by gently sliding it to and fro until the glue cooled and the block became immovable. Many of these glue blocks are as solid today as the day they were made, but today's craftsmen should realize that these animal glues may crystallize, especially in contemporary desert-dry heated apartments. At the other extreme, they have very little resistance to moisture. To sum it up, we may say that it is inconvenient to use, may be loosened by shock or vibration, and offers little resistance to dampness. The fact that it dries brown is its only asset.

A very satisfactory adhesive for general woodworking is one of the many synthetic polyvinal resin adhesives available in most hardware stores. One of the best is Elmer's glue, which comes in handy plastic squeeze bottles and is instantly available for use. Chemists have worked diligently to develop a ready-to-use adhesive that will set at a temperature of 70 degrees or warmer and which will create a strong, moisture-resistant bond. These glues are recommended wherever you have a sufficiently large area to make a good glue bond and where the wood is clean and freshly cut. When set, these resin adhesives are clear, which is an asset if you are making modern or contemporary furniture. But for assembly of woods that will later be stained to resemble the natural patina of two-hundred-year-old wood, the preferred glue is one with brown pigment added. With a brown adhesive, glue lines are less evident and one can see the squeezed-out glue prior to sanding and staining these areas (see Sources, 12).

Within the past few years chemists have developed a new and extremely strong epoxy adhesive that does not rely on the absorption or evaporation of moisture to make a bond which is thoroughly waterproof. This somewhat more expensive two-part adhesive, consisting of a glue and a catalyst (or hardener), is available in most hardware stores. It is important that the directions for mixing and using be followed exactly. The glue should be used in a well-ventilated area and your hands should be washed thoroughly after using. Epoxy adhesives are recommended for making repairs where a previous glue has failed. In

Glues and Gluing

making such repairs, it is very important to remove all the old glue before applying the epoxy. These chemical glues are about the only adhesives which can be used to make a satisfactory end grain bond. Wipe off the glue squeezed out and don't try to mask your joints unless you remove the tape before the glue has finally set. These epoxy glues come in various speeds of hardening, varying from five minutes up to two hours or more.

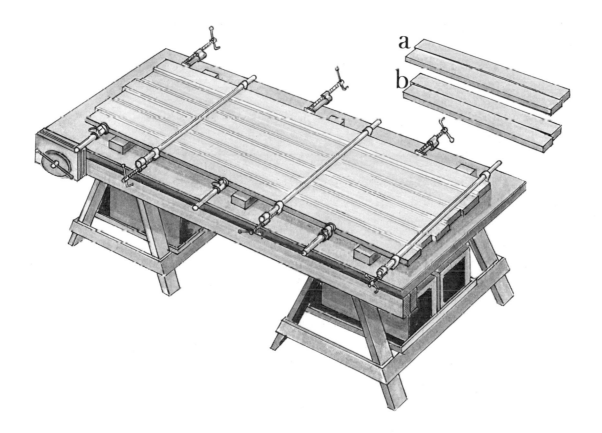

Another type of adhesive, which offers considerable help in special cases where strong bonds are sought and where it may be difficult or impossible to supply sustained clamping pressure, is contact cement. This adhesive requires coating both surfaces that are to be brought together, with each surface allowed to dry until it becomes nontacky. Although

Glues and Gluing

the surfaces are nontacky to the touch, they are extremely tacky to each other. In bringing the two surfaces together, they should be separated by hard-surfaced paper until the two parts are precisely positioned with relation to each other. The separating paper can then be gently slid from between so that the two coated surfaces come together. It is extremely difficult to separate or adjust the parts once contact has been made. If smoothly sanded surfaces are lightly coated (a light second coat may be desirable where an extra strong bond is desired) and allowed to dry they may be put together with very little sign of the joint.

As a weak link spoils the chain, so an improperly made glue joint may be the undoing of an otherwise fine piece of furniture. To make glue joints that are as strong as the wood itself, it is necessary to follow a few commonsense rules.

Gluing should always be done in a warm, dry area.

As stated earlier, the wood to be glued should have a moisture content of 8 percent or less. If it has more moisture than this, it may very well crack or open in the joints at a later date. If you do not know the moisture content of your boards, but feel that they have been well dried out of doors and under cover, let them equalize for a few days (or longer, if possible) in a warm, dry area prior to jointing and gluing; it is important that each board have the same moisture content before gluing.

The edges of boards to be glued should be jointed with care so that they will be in contact in all areas when the joint is glued and under pressure. Sometimes jointed edges will be "bowed," as shown at *a* in the detail. If the ends of adjacent boards touch when assembled without pressure, and the center of the joint shows a slight opening, this will be a joint of great strength. However, the center opening should not be so great that clamp pressure will not bring the glued surfaces together. If the edges are bowed, as shown at *b*, the joint will be completely unsatisfactory.

Adhesive need be applied to only one edge being glued. Once glue has been applied to an edge, the panel should be under clamp pressure within five minutes. If the glue is allowed to set too long before clamping glue will penetrate the pores of the wood and a "starved," or weak, joint will result. The strongest glue lines are thin ones.

46

Surfacing Wood

THERE ARE TWO ESSENTIALS for pleasurably and satisfactorily smoothing and surfacing a board or a glued-up panel: a stable, solid, flat surface on which to clamp the piece on which you are working (see A Workbench, pages 19–21) and a supersharp cutting edge. There is a very real thrill in the feel of a razor-sharp plane removing a hair-thin uniform shaving of wood.

It is not easy to develop a perfect edge on a cutting tool and some craftsmen prefer to have a number of plane blades and chisels which can be taken or mailed to professional sharpening shops as the edges become worn or, as will sometimes happen, nicked. An alternative is to invest in such sharpening accessories as a double-faced oilstone (coarse and fine), a superfine oilstone (Arkansas Washita), a chisel and plane-blade sharpening holder (see Sources, 1, 2), and finally, a good piece of oil- and rouge-impregnated sole leather on which to hone the final edge. A thin oil should be used on the oilstone during sharpening. A good woodworking project is to make a box in which to house the oilstones, which should be kept clean and uncontaminated. Strips of wood slightly more than half the thickness of the stone can be tacked around the perimeter of a piece of board to make a depression into which the stone will fit snugly, with a duplicate to serve as a cover.

If the tool has been nicked or if the edge is not at right angles to the sides, it may need to be ground straight on a grinding wheel. If so, care must be taken not to "burn" the cutting edge by holding it too forcefully or too long against the wheel, thereby removing the temper of the steel. Frequent immersion in a small dish of cold water during grinding will help prevent burning. If you have your own sharpening accessories, frequent touch-ups of the cutting edge are better than waiting until the tool is hopelessly dull.

Early craftsmen, either because of limited sharpening equipment or in order to make planing a little easier, sometimes used a scrub plane, whose cutting edge was slightly curved, or "brought back," across its width (a). This produced a hand-planed look that is sometimes desired today.

Nothing will dull a plane blade quicker than abrasives such as dried glue. Remove such glue residue or squeeze-out from the surface of the panel using a high-speed hacksaw blade with its ends wrapped in masking tape to make handles (b). Either the teeth or the back edge of the blade should be used alternately to remove every trace of dried glue before planing. These high-speed blades cost only a few cents more than regular blades and their superior steel will hold up much longer (see Sources, 1, 2).

47

Surfacing Wood

Before planing, make stops (*c*) from stock somewhat thinner than the board or panel to be surfaced. Clamp the work to the bench so that it will be restrained from sliding. In planing the surface of a panel in which some boards extend above the others, it is best to make diagonal strokes as indicated until the board is of uniform thickness. A "scrub" plane with

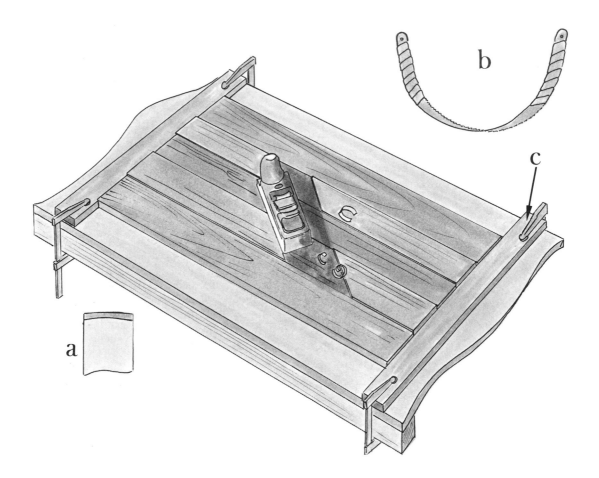

a rounded edge, as mentioned above, is best for this work. The old-fashioned wood-bodied planes are well suited to this work, because their lignum-vitae shoes provide natural lubrication during planing (see Sources, 1).

Surfacing Wood

Final planing should be with a "jointer" plane, in the direction of the grain of the wood, using either a straight or rounded blade, depending upon the effect desired. The blade must be sharp and the shaving thin. Don't be overanxious to make the final surface look as though it were surfaced by a power-driven planer; the uneven effect of the handmade tabletop is much more rewarding.

The planed surface should be lightly sanded with 4-0 paper or cloth wrapped around a block of wood.

Sawing to Shape

ARLY CRAFTSMEN did not restrict themselves to straight-line forms of woodworking despite the absence of power-driven jigsaws, band saws and the modern saber saw. Graceful curves contributed to the utility and beauty of their work, whether it was the embellishment of a simple set of shelves or the aesthetically pleasing shape of the whale weather vane.

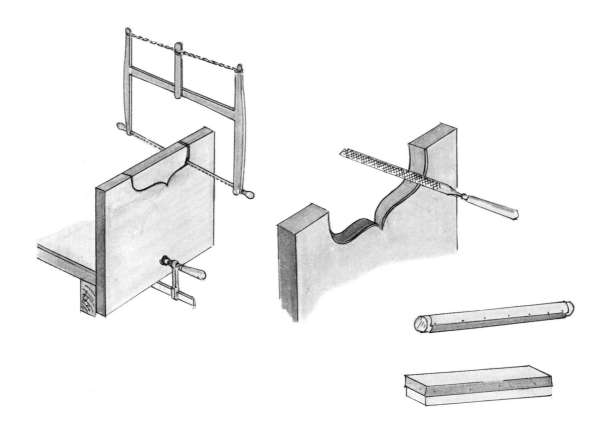

Never underestimate the value of the eighteenth-century bow saw. It does the work of a power-operated band saw, is safe for beginners, and is easily portable. A turn of the swivel handles rotates the blade so that the cutting teeth can be kept in the direction the curve is taking. A tourniquet tightens the blade and holds it in position while the saw is being used.

Sawing to Shape

The curve to be cut should be carefully traced so as to be identically spaced on both sides of the stock, which should be held firmly in a vice or clamped to the top of a workbench. If the design to be cut does not meet the outside edge (so that the cut may be started there), you must bore a small hole in the "waste" part. To do this, dismount the bow saw blade, insert it through the hole, and reconnect it in the frame. It is important that the saw blade be kept perpendicular to the faces of the stock, and the cut should be checked frequently to be sure that it is following the pattern traced on each side of the stock. If it does not, it means that the saw is not being held straight and perpendicular. The saw cut should be kept close to but strictly on the "waste" side of the traced design.

The finished cut should be carefully dressed to conform exactly to the traced design and may be done in two steps. First, the edge can be rough-shaped to the finish line by removing the excess wood with a cabinet rasp. One of the best of these is called a four-in-hand file (sometimes called a shoe rasp) with flat and half-round faces, including coarse and fine cutting surfaces (see Sources, 1). Final smoothing can be achieved by wrapping a piece of 4-0 sanding cloth or paper around a block or a dowel as shown.

Making Breadboard Ends

Early craftsmen were thoroughly knowledgeable about the characteristics of wood. They knew that wet or unseasoned wood shrank considerably across the grain while drying, but that it hardly changed at all in the direction of the grain. They knew that even thoroughly dried wood has a tendency to "come and go" across the grain with changes in humidity. Their wide boards, when properly seasoned, were a natural for tabletops. To protect the vulnerable end grain of pine planks from possible damage, they installed what we today call breadboard ends. These strips, matching the tabletops in width and thickness,

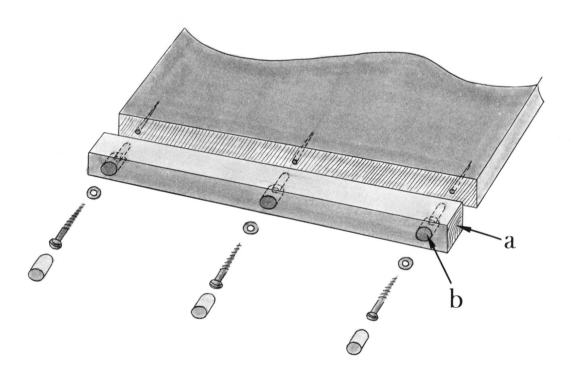

were fastened to the tops with wooden pins or hand-forged nails. These somewhat loose-fitting fastenings allowed for seasonal, across-the-grain changes in the wood. It was not until centuries later that these tops showed evidence of cracking when introduced to the dry atmosphere of the overheated contemporary home.

If you are lucky enough to resurrect an antique wide board from some attic or if you

Making Breadboard Ends

fabricate your own wide panel by gluing together boards of good clear modern pine, you will want to carry on the tradition and apply breadboard ends to your tabletop. In deference to the extremes of atmospheric moisture which accompany modern living, you will need to provide some extra leeway in fastening the ends to your tabletop. This is accomplished by providing a loose fit for the screws you will use to fasten the breadboard end across the width of the tabletop.

This end cleat (*a*) should be approximately twice as wide as it is thick and should be drilled with several holes (*b*), each to a depth of approximately ½ inch. Each hole should be of sufficient diameter (preferably ½ inch) to accept a washer, which will be placed under the head of a panhead (or roundheaded) screw, which, in turn, will be used to fasten the end board to the tabletop. Drill in the bottom of each of these holes (and in the center) a smaller hole of ¼-inch diameter; this hole should be drilled through the cleat. A number 8 panhead steel "tapping" screw is best suited to end-grain use. After inserting both the washer and the screw in each hole and after positioning the end cleat, the screws should be driven approximately 1 inch into the tabletop.

After the cleat has been fastened in place, the ½-inch holes should be glued, plugged with a short hardwood dowel, and sanded smooth.

Making Tapered Legs

HAVE YOU ADMIRED graceful tapered legs like those of the Wayside Inn table on page 86? These legs are tapered on two sides only; the outer faces are vertical to the floor. In a length of 24 inches, they taper from $1\frac{5}{8}$ inches at the top to $\frac{7}{8}$ inch at the bottom. Such tapers can be made easily on your table saw.

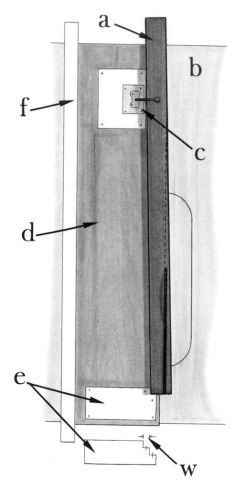

The secret is to make a simple jig to hold the stock (*a*) while it is being pushed through the saw, which removes a wedge-shaped slice. It is important that the leg stock be dry, straight, square, and smooth. The best stock to use is rock maple. With a pencil, outline

Making Tapered Legs

on the leg stock the "cut line" or the shape of the tapered wedge to be sawed; this is shown in the drawing as a dotted line.

The base of the jig (d) should be made from a planed board or a piece of plywood about ¾ inch thick with parallel edges, 5 or 6 inches wide, and about the length of the stock to be tapered. With the saw blade raised slightly above the table surface (b), position the baseboard so that one of its long edges is against the fence (f) and the other about ⅛ inch from the saw face, adjusting the fence as necessary. From two small pieces of wood ¾ inch thick, cut clamp and step blocks, c and e respectively. Both of these blocks should be screwed to the baseboard, where they will act as registers to hold the leg stock in alignment while it is being worked. A toggle clamp, shown at c, will be fastened to the clamp block. The step block should be made with a small notch, square on each edge and cut in one corner. A steel brad, driven into the notch and with its head subsequently filed to a sharp point, will help in securing the leg while it is being sawed.

To align the leg stock for sawing, center it lengthwise on the baseboard and screw the clamp and step blocks so that the cut line is directly above the saw blade and parallel to the edge of the baseboard.

Once the adjustments are complete, remove the jig from the table and raise the saw to the desired height. Keep in mind that a planer saw will make the smoothest cut. You are now ready to cut off the wedge.

After cutting, turn the stock so that the sawed surface is facing up; make the second cut. The setting of the fence is not changed between the cutting of tapers.

For those who may wish to make a leg that is tapered on all four sides, make a step block with two steps, as shown in the detail. The distance (w) between the steps should be the equivalent of the thickness of the wedge to be removed, as measured at the leg bottom. The first two cuts should be made in the first step, as explained above; the second and third cuts are made in the second step. Be sure to drive brads into the steps, as before, to hold the leg bottom. A small hole drilled in the leg bottom, the diameter of the brad, will improve the latter's holding power.

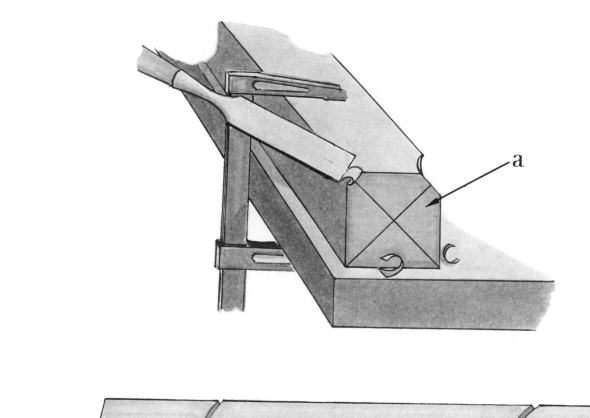

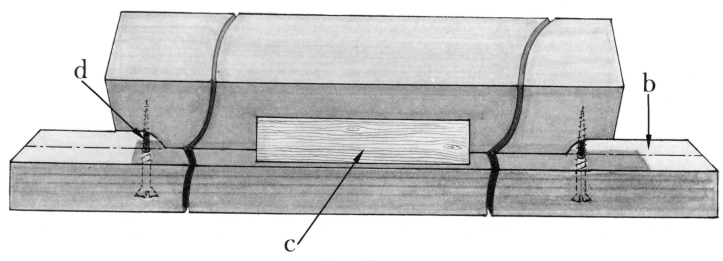

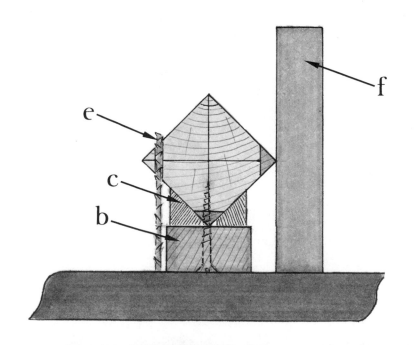

Making Octagonal Legs

Leg stock should be of dry, straight hardwood with four square faces. It should be about 1½ inches longer than the finished leg. The ends should be cut square. On one end of the stock draw diagonal lines (*a*). At both ends of the stock and on the same two adjacent corners, chisel the edges away as shown with a bite about ¼ inch deep and ¾ inch long. These will be used as entry points for the hold-down screws which will support the stock while sawing.

Make a guide block (*b*) from a piece of flat hardwood stock surfaced on both faces to about ¾ inch in thickness and a little less than the width of the leg stock. Draw a center line on the top face of the guide block as shown.

From good straight stock, cut two 45-degree wedges, triangular in cross section and about 8 inches long (*c*). A pair of these wedges, placed side by side as shown, should occupy a space about the width of the guide block. These should be accurately nailed or glued to the guide block so that the 45-degree edges are closely and precisely mounted along the center line. Contact cement is good for this purpose. If the leg stock is fairly long, use a pair of these blocks near each end instead of in the center as shown. Use a square to make sure that a diagonal line on the end of the leg is perpendicular to the guide block.

Temporarily, clamp the leg stock to the guide block with one edge of the leg along the center line. Drill screw holes through the guide block and into the corner notches of the leg stock. Drive the screws (*d*) and remove the clamps.

Set the saw blade (*e*) to the correct height. With the fence (*f*) at the required distance from the saw and using one edge of the leg stock as a guide against the fence, make a cut as shown. Move the fence as required and make a similar second cut after turning the guide block end-on-end. It is possible to make the seventh and eighth faces of the octagonal leg eliminating the guide block and using the previously made faces as bearings, but in the interest of safety it is best to use the guide block as before.

Boring Seat and Leg Holes

I F THE CHARM of the work center which you have created and the joy of potential creativity are as infectious as they are to most craftsmen, you will be spending many fleeting hours at your workbench. Welcome partners for these times will be a couple of stools such as those copied from originals in the Parson Capen House shown on page 76.

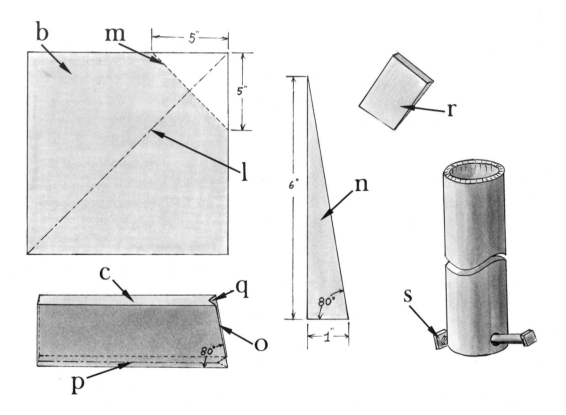

The construction of pieces like these involves creating octagonal legs as shown on the last two pages, fabricating a few jigs, and making a simple device for producing a tenon on the end of each leg. Each of these accessories is relatively easy to make and will be a useful and permanent addition to your shop.

Let us assume that you have glued up a stool top about 14 inches square and approximately 1¾ inches thick, or that you have been fortunate enough to find a block of well-

Boring Seat and Leg Holes

seasoned pine from which to cut one. Let us assume, also, that you have sawed the octagonal legs that will be needed.

Your first step will be to lay out, on top of the stool, the centers for the four holes into which the leg tenons will be inserted. With a pencil, draw two diagonal lines across the top from corner to corner. At their point of intersection, using a compass, swing a circle of about an 11-inch diameter. The intersections of the circle with the diagonals will be the centers of the legs.

To drill the holes for the leg tenons, it will be necessary to construct a simple jig to support the drilling bit at the proper angle while cutting; the tops for both the high and low stools may be drilled at the sample angle. The base (b) for the jig is a piece of ½-inch-thick plywood about 12 inches square. Draw a line (l) between two opposite corners; this diagonal will later be used to position the drilling guide block. Draw a line (m), located as shown. Saw along m and discard the triangle.

The drill guide (c) will be part of the drilling jig and is made from a block of hardwood approximately 10 inches long, 4 inches wide, and 1 inch thick. This block should be machined straight and square. To prepare for an angle cut on one end of this block, draw a right triangle (n) on a piece of cardboard. Cut out the triangle with a scissors. Using this pattern, draw an 80-degree bevel on the end of the block (o).

Saw the block along o and discard the triangular piece. Draw a center line (p) on the longest face of the block as shown. Using the table saw with the arbor tilted to 45 degrees, cut a V groove on the slanted end (q). With screws and glue, fasten this block to the base (b) so that the center line of the block is superimposed on the center line of the base and so that the apex of the V groove just touches the end of the diagonal line (l) as shown.

With the seat-boring bit tight against the V groove, adjust the drill jig on the stool top so that the spur of the bit will be located at the intersection of the circle and one of the diagonals. Adjust the drilling jig so that the diagonal line of the jig also lies on one of the seat-top diagonals. In addition, it may be well to position a piece of plywood or wood (w) about ¾ inch thick and about the same size as the base (b) beneath the stool top so that the bit, as it penetrates the stool top, will not splinter the pine. When ready for drilling, the above sandwich of materials — the jig base (b), the stool top (a), and the panel (w) — will all be clamped to a corner of the workbench as shown on the next page. With the bit-brace holding a well-sharpened bit tight against the V groove, bore a hole for a leg tenon.

Boring Seat and Leg Holes

Move and adjust the jig to bore similar holes at other intersections of the circle and diagonals. (For these large-diameter bits, see Sources, 1.)

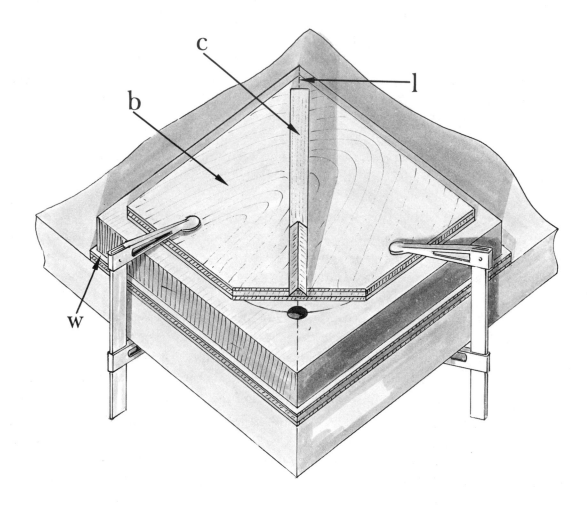

To make a tenon on an end of each of the octagonal legs, begin by drawing a circle on an end the diameter of a seat hole. A fifty-cent piece is helpful in drawing a 1¼-inch circle, a twenty-five-cent piece makes a 1-inch circle; each of these coins allows for the pencil line.

Boring Seat and Leg Holes

Measure back from the end of this leg a distance of 2 inches. With a sharp knife or the edge of a file, mark a line on the circumference of the stock at this point. With the leg clamped firmly to the workbench and using a rasp or four-in-hand file, round the end of the leg to the tenon diameter desired over the 2-inch distance, but do not go under the desired diameter.

Another useful tool that you can make is now needed. Obtain from your plumber a piece of iron pipe that is 10 inches long and with an inside diameter of $1\frac{1}{4}$ inches, or whatever is needed. Make sure that at least one end of this pipe has been cut off with a pipe cutter rather than a hacksaw; the former leaves a sharp cut on the inside edge of the pipe. With a good round backfile and emery cloth, smooth the inside edge of the sharp cut to remove any burrs. Remove any oil residue from the pipe inside and out. Near the other end of the pipe drill a $\frac{1}{2}$-inch hole into which a bolt or rod can be inserted, as shown at *s*.

Into the sharp end of this pipe, or tenon shaper, drive the rasped end of the leg about $\frac{1}{2}$ inch. Remove the pipe from the leg and file down the excess wood on the tenon so that the leg can be driven with ease another $\frac{1}{2}$ inch. Repeat this operation until the entire 2 inches can be readily driven into the pipe. The rod or bolt inserted in the pipe will assist in turning or driving off the pipe during the tenoning operation. It is, of course, essential that the central axis of the pipe be kept in alignment with the axis of the leg to guarantee that the tenon will be in line with the leg. It may be necessary to sand the finished tenon slightly to give it a snug fit in the seat hole.

Position four legs in a seat. Place a straightedge across any two adjacent legs, lining up the flat surfaces with it; turn the legs as needed. You may wish to prepare the underside of the seat to receive the leg tenons as shown in detail on page 77. This counterboring is a fine touch, but it contributes little to the strength of the stools. Once positioned, mark the location and number of each leg under the seat and close to where they enter the seat, so that the legs can be removed and returned to the same exact position. With the stool standing on the workbench, scribe the lower ends of the legs and cut them so that they rest firmly on the surface. Scribe a line around the extension of the tenons above the upper surface of the stool top. Remove each leg, saw off the excess (leaving the pencil line), and reposition the leg in the stool top. With sandpaper wrapped about a block of wood, sand the ends of each of the tenons in the stool even with the top surface; sanding should be done in the direction of the grain of the pine.

Boring Seat and Leg Holes

With a pencil, continue the line of the diagonals across the ends of the legs. These lines mark the cuts for the wedges that will later be driven into the tenons. Remove the legs from the top and, with each leg firmly clamped in a vise or to the workbench, make a slot for the wedge about 1½ inches deep and along the axis of the leg.

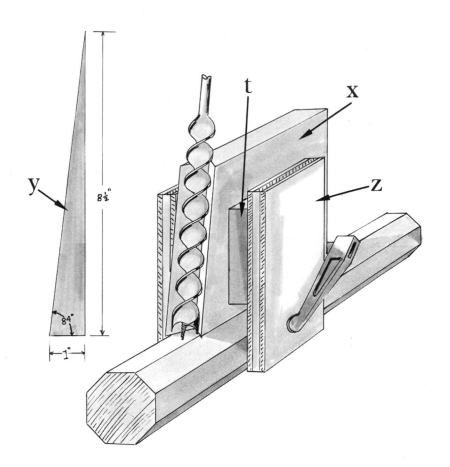

You must now prepare to drill holes for the dowels, or stretchers, of the high stool. The dowels will give strength and rigidity to the legs in which they are inserted. On adjacent flat faces of the legs, mark the centers of the holes to be drilled.

Boring Seat and Leg Holes

Another jig should now be made similar to the one already constructed, except that the guide block (x) should be made with a drilling angle of 84 degrees. To arrive at the proper angle, make a pattern as sketched (y). Two pieces (z) of $\frac{1}{2}$-inch plywood measuring about 4 inches square and two filler blocks (t) as needed should be glued to the sides as shown (x), completing the drilling jig.

Position a $\frac{3}{4}$-inch bit in the V groove of the jig so that the spur point is on the center of a dowel hole to be drilled and clamp the pieces (z) to the leg as shown. In turn, clamp the leg to be drilled to the workbench. Drill each hole about $\frac{5}{8}$ inch deep; an ink mark on the bit can act as a depth gauge. Drill the remaining holes in like manner. Cut $\frac{7}{8}$-inch hardwood dowels to the necessary lengths (dowels are available at most lumberyards) and shape the ends to fit the drilled holes. Make wedges of hardwood as shown at r, with the grain of the wood parallel to the long dimension.

When all the holes have been bored and the dowels fitted, you are ready to assemble the stool. Coat the walls of the seat and leg holes with adhesive. Assemble the dowels in the legs and the tenons in the seat holes. Pull the legs against the dowels by making a loop of strong cord around all four legs; the rope may be tightened by twisting a screwdriver in the cord. As the tourniquet gets tighter, the legs will go farther into their holes. A gentle tapping with a pine block will assist in this assembly. With a paper towel, wipe off the glue squeezed out. Apply a spot of glue to the slots and drive in each of the four wedges. When the glue is dry, cut off any remaining extension of the wedges and sand the seat top as before. Round the upper edges of the seat and corners.

Although the steps outlined here referred specifically to the construction of stools, the jigs and fixures suggested can be modified for the construction of benches and chairs.

Finishing

IN THE BEGINNING, from sheer necessity, the colonists were certainly far more concerned about building a house and barn to keep out the weather than they were with protecting these structures from the ravages of the future. Furniture, too, was built to be functional and was often used in the raw, with tabletops scoured to whiteness with sand and strong handmade soap. The friction of daily use, fireplace smoke, and perhaps an occasional application of beeswax enhanced the natural mellowing of benches, chairs, and chests to produce the patina that we aspire to achieve today.

With the passage of time, the innate artistic urges of the colonists surfaced and took form in a wide variety of ways. They developed finishes and designs using pigmented colors and natural dye stains. Probably the first experiments on surface finishes, either for protection or beauty, made use of casein from sour milk from cheese making and easily accessible pigments such as natural blue clay or ground brick dust. Later, iron oxide, copper sulfate, yellow ocher, and red lead provided richer and more varied colors. Paints of this type, with a history tracing back to the ancient Hebrews, were sturdy and durable as anyone who has tried to remove some of these finishes from an antique can attest to.

Linseed oil came into use in Europe in the fifteenth century as a paint base. Since flax was a staple among the American colonists and linseed was one of its by-products, its early use on these shores is understandable. It was distributed by itinerant peddlers using animal bladders as containers. Although its function was primarily as an exterior paint base, it was used to treat some kitchen furniture that would otherwise have remained unfinished. It was this oil finish that became so devastatingly popular in the 1920s, when everyone with a beautifully painted heirloom wanted to dip it in lye to live a new life, with all the grain exposed. Too late we have realized what a desecration this was.

It came to be the style to paint Windsors and settees a dark green. Samuel Wing, a cabinetmaker in Sandwich, Massachusetts, around 1797, finished many of his Windsors in a "goode green color." On occasion, tables were painted blue and the backs of cupboards a light brick red. Using these and a range of other pigmented colors suspended in either skim milk or stale beer, itinerant painters decorated furniture such as the pine chest found in the historic Lincoln House and shown on page 96.

Little of the luxury of wallpaper, imported from France and very expensive, was available away from the cities to brighten up the country farmhouse. Artistic expression in the form of stencils, cut from parchment, together with "earth" colors provided borders and

Finishing

designs to relieve the dullness of plastered walls that were commonly finished in flat oyster, white, or parchment shades.

Perhaps, without knowing it, the early colonists set a decorating trend. It is still in the best of taste to paint room trim, the interior of cupboards, and perhaps an occasional table to match.

Fortunately, there are many fine paints available today that duplicate these old colors. If you use an oil paint, get one with finely ground color pigments. These cost a bit more but you will use fewer coats to achieve complete coverage, and the fewer the coats the more durable the finish. When applying a paint finish, be sure that the wood fibers have been sealed. When paint is applied directly to the wood, the fibers absorb the oil medium in which the pigments have been dispersed, leaving a concentration of pigments on the surface. The result of this concentration is a brittle finish that will crack when dented. Paint applied to a surface that has been primed will be much more flexible and far less likely to chip. To get the old "skim milk" look on wood trim, specify a paint with a dull, eggshell finish. Such paint is almost flat in appearance, but is still washable.

Much of the success of a good paint job lies in the preparation of the surface. If you are repainting, prepare the surface by washing well with a soap-free agent. A thrifty New England saying is, Washing is as good as a coat of paint. When dry, scrape and fill cracks where necessary and sand with 4-0 paper to remove as much of the old loose paint as possible. Sanding will also allow the oils in the new paint to penetrate into the old surface. In preparation for painting, wipe the sanded surface with a damp rag to remove the sandpaper dust.

If paint is to be applied to a new surface, sand the wood so that it is uniformly smooth and follow this with an undercoat, or primer, which, in turn, should be sanded when dry. Where there are knots in the wood, prime these areas with shellac to prevent sap bleedthrough.

For best results, painting should be done in a warm, dry room. A fine-bristled brush should be used. It will spread the paint more evenly and will hold the paint better during application.

We, as present-day craftsmen, are not handicapped by the shortages and restrictions that our predecessors overcame so manfully, and we can choose between a painted or natural stain finish with greater ease.

Finishing

To achieve a centuries-old look, modern chemists have developed oil stains, water stains, and alcohol stains — tobacco stains have even been recommended by some.

The clear, rich colors of oil stains and the ease with which they can be used to cover large areas uniformly make them among the best stain finishes for amateur use. To come as close as possible to the two-hundred-year-old look, predominantly brown stains are recommended. These stains, usually made with oil-dye pigments suspended in a base of boiled linseed oil, turpentine, and driers in ready-mixed form, may be either brushed or ragged over the clean bare wood (Sources, 8.)

From five to ten minutes after applying the stain, rag the surface free of all residue, wiping in the direction of the grain of the wood. Areas in which glue has penetrated and that were missed in the sanding operation may appear as light spots. These should be sanded while the stain is wet and more stain applied. During the twenty-four hours it takes for these stains to dry, they penetrate the surface wood fibers and even provide some protection for the wood surface. The amount of stain to be applied to any particular surface and the interval before wiping can best be determined by experimenting on a scrap of similar wood or the underside of, say, a tabletop. The colors of these stains fade with age, yielding to the natural warm hues and patina that only time and nature can produce.

If a darker color is desired, a coat of darker oil stain may be applied over the first coat after it has dried thoroughly. A darker stain may be made by adding burnt umber or Vandyke brown, available in small tubes at most hardware and paint stores. If, after the second application, the stain appears too dark, it may be lightened by ragging the surface with turpentine while the stain is still wet.

There is always an exception to any rule and one has to be made for an occasional piece of extra-hard rock maple that may seem to defy attempts at penetration using an oil stain. In such cases a base coat of brown water stain will give the penetration and color needed. Once this water stain has dried, the surface is rubbed lightly with 4-0 steel wool and an oil stain applied to achieve the final color desired.

Although I have commented favorably on oil stains, I should point out that some professional wood finishers feel that there are no better stains than water stains, which are easily made by combining dry aniline powder, which comes in a number of colors, with boiling water. Such stains are low in cost, have a stable shelf life, and can be mixed to produce your own desired shade.

Finishing

Water stains have the disadvantage of tending to "raise the grain" of the wood to produce a slightly fuzzy surface. This can be remedied after the color has been achieved by applying a coat of sanding sealer to harden the fuzz, which can be easily smoothed by sanding when dry. Some finishers prefer to prepare the surface of the wood before staining by thoroughly wetting it with clear water, allowing it to dry, and then sanding the surface before applying the water stain itself. Even with this preparation, the use of a sanding sealer and smooth sanding after staining are desirable. For water-staining large areas, use a wide, full-bristled brush and apply the stain rapidly with a well-wetted brush in long strokes in the direction of the grain of the wood. If overlap streaks appear, they can be blended while wet using a separate brush with clear water or diluted stain. It is not recommended that water stains be used on wood from which old finish has been stripped, since the pores of the wood have undoubtedly been filled so that the stain will not penetrate.

Alcohol, or spirit, stains are also popular. They are a mixture of alcohol, benzine, turpentine, and coloring dye. Since they dry very rapidly they are useful as touch-up stains and may have a special appeal to craftsmen who are pressed for time. Because of their rapid drying it becomes almost impossible to use them for staining large areas, for overlaps are likely to be decidedly darker than the normal color. Also, spirit stains do not penetrate deeply and a scratched surface will reveal the color of the underlying wood.

Whereas eastern white pine and most hardwoods are relatively easy to finish with stains, more porous woods such as western sugar and ponderosa pine require special attention. Prior to staining, these woods should be primed with a stain sealer or wood stabilizer. Without stabilization before staining, the porous wood may appear to be blotchy where variable penetration of the stain has left a concentration of color pigments. Exposed end grain should also be treated as porous wood and stabilized before staining. Once stabilized, the surface can be treated as a nonporous wood and stained accordingly. This stabilizer, or primer, can be made easily by thinning a sanding sealer with mineral spirits on a 1:1 ratio.

If you are contemplating a finish for a room in which you want to impart the same shade of stain to paneling, window trim, and wall cabinets, and there is a chance that the woodwork is a combination of many types of pine or other woods, the best approach may be to stabilize the entire surface, sanding lightly before staining. Whenever possible, first finish leftover scraps of the various woods or a small area in an inconspicuous place to see whether you will like the result before going ahead with the entire room.

Finishing

There are several protective coatings which can be applied over a stain finish. Of these, a wax coating is the simplest to apply. One of the most desirable waxes is one made with Carnauba wax, imported from Brazil. This wax imparts a durable surface that can be readily refreshed from time to time by subsequent coats. Any finish will be subject to scarring, but the wax is easiest to repair. This is the finish subscribed to by those who feel that the least finish is the best finish.

For those who prefer a finish with more depth and body than can be obtained with plain stain or oil, a flat varnish coating applied over the stain is most pleasing. Varnish, when dry, may be rubbed with a mixture of boiled linseed oil and turpentine, mixed half and half. A rag dipped into this mixture should be used to pick up some finely ground pumice from a shallow dish. Rub this oil and abrasive mix into the surface of the varnish until a smooth sheen is obtained; then rag off the residue so that the remaining film is indiscernible. Any appreciable amount of oil left on the surface may not dry in your lifetime, or so it seems. When the oil surface is dry, which should take a week or so, it may be followed up with successive thin coats of oil and turpentine at two-week intervals, as long as your patience lasts.

Remember that the finish you are applying will tend to slow down the absorption of moisture from the air into the pores of the wood and will therefore reduce the swelling and shrinking that occur with atmospheric changes. Because of this, it is important to finish all the surfaces of the wood, such as the underside of a tabletop, the inside of drawers, etc. A wood panel that is finished on one side only will absorb moisture into the unfinished face, and this face will expand, causing warping of the panel.

Finishing should be done in a dry, warm room. After finishing, be sure to discard all stain- and oil-soaked rags — by either burning or storing in a metal container outside — to avoid the possibility of spontaneous combustion.

The finish of your completed reproduction should complement its design. A dull stain finish is in keeping with simple country pine furniture. A "flyspeck" finish, of doubtful authenticity, seems to be honored in the best department stores, but is hardly exemplary of good seventeenth-century housekeeping.

Keep in mind that flat varnish should be kept well stirred while it is being used. If the "flattening" agent is not evenly dispersed in the varnish, the final finish may be uneven or glossy rather than flat. The driers and solvents in most of these finishes will evaporate rather rapidly if there is the minutest opening in the container while in storage. To prevent

Finishing

this, store your cans upsidedown on a piece of newspaper to make sure that the seal is really tight.

Now a word about cleaning brushes, for even the cheapest brush should be cleaned instead of being discarded. Rinse the brush in a little thinner in a shallow dish and wipe it as dry as possible with an old rag. Wash the brush with warm water and soap to remove the residue, wipe it dry with a paper towel, and then wrap the bristles in a normal position so that they will be ready for the next painting. Do not stand a brush on its bristles.

I feel certain that many readers, particularly those who like to "brew their own," will disagree with at least some of my suggestions for finishing. I have even had correspondence with a lady who says she prefers tobacco juice over all other stains. It has occurred to me to ask her how she handles the large quids, but I have never quite gotten up the courage.

Decorating with Folk Art

FOLK ART was a natural expression of the colonists, who created fanciful as well as life-like artifacts based on objects that were part of their environment. Uninhibited by any formal artistic training, they had free rein to create such practical and decorative works as prancing horse weather vanes, and chests and tinware embellished with birds and floral motifs.

You may wish to emulate these anonymous early American craftsmen and create your own art forms, or you may literally "borrow a page from their books" by reproducing the exact designs that have come down to us and which are displayed in your library's reference books.

What a colorful and imaginative addition to a colonial American setting can be made with a pine piece decorated with a horse and rider in the Pennsylvania Dutch style or leaves on "chandelier" branches popular in Guilford, Connecticut, in the 1600s. These motifs can be found in the *Index of American Design* (The Smithsonian), *American Arts and Skills* (Life), *American Folk Art* (Dover), and *History of Colonial Antiques* (American Heritage). These and other colorfully illustrated books are undoubtedly in your library. With very little effort you can transfer these designs to many pieces shown in the back of this book.

It is easy to see that the originators of these paintings, done in gay "earth" colors such as chrome yellow, Indian red, and indigo blue, brought the joy of artistic expression to the lives of their contemporaries. The motifs of many of these decorations have an almost childlike simplicity and their originators were often itinerant decorators who were not concerned with the niceties of technique. You too need not be concerned with an exact duplication of color or detail of line.

To make these transfers, a relatively inexpensive tool that will be helpful is a pantagraph, a device for enlarging or reducing drawings and designs (see Sources, 10). With it you can make copies of paintings and patterns in the numerous reference books in any desired size. Many libraries have available copying machines that can provide you with a good black and white copy of almost any page in any book; the design you choose should be thus copied for use with the pantagraph.

This apparatus consists of two pairs of wooden bars with numbered holes. These bars are fastened to one another with screw eyes in different positions, depending upon the size of the enlargement desired. Fasten your black and white copy to a hard smooth surface to-

Decorating with Folk Art

gether with a sheet of plain white paper large enough to accept the enlarged copy. Using the blunt end of the tracer point of the pantagraph, follow the outline of the design of the copy from the book while a soft pencil in the other leg transfers the enlarged design to the plain paper, as shown. When this drawing is complete, mount it securely with carbon paper,

face down, on the piece of furniture on which you wish to paint the design. Trace over the lines of the enlarged drawing with a pencil, creating carbon lines on the wood surface.

Decorating with Folk Art

Having established the pattern of the design, you may fill in the various colored areas by hand with fine-pointed paintbrushes, or you may find it easier and more accurate to outline the areas of different colors with a "paint-striping" tool, subsequently filling in these areas with a brush. One of the most versatile of these tools consists of a small glass vial that contains the paint, on the open end of which is screwed a "roller head" equipped with a knurled wheel. These stripers are available in widths from $\frac{1}{64}$ up to $\frac{1}{4}$ inch (see Sources, 9). The wheel is rolled along the outline of any given color and will make a smooth, accurate line such as would formerly have required the services of an experienced and accomplished "striper" with a sable brush. It will be necessary to clean the vial and roller carefully between each color application.

Be sure to let all background areas dry before striping and allow each adjacent color to dry well before applying a different contiguous color. Striping errors can be corrected easily by wiping off the errant wet lines with a rag dipped in turpentine. Paints designated as "flat-eggshell" come closest to duplicating the dull sheen of the old sour-milk "earth" colors.

THE REPRODUCTIONS

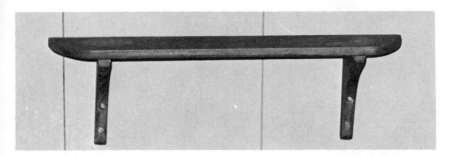

Shaker Shelf

The pure and simple lines of this pine Shaker shelf make it as functional today as it was a century and a half ago. Originally, these shelves held the personal effects of those living and working in the Shaker dwellings. They were usually attached solidly to the wall beneath the ever-present pegboards.

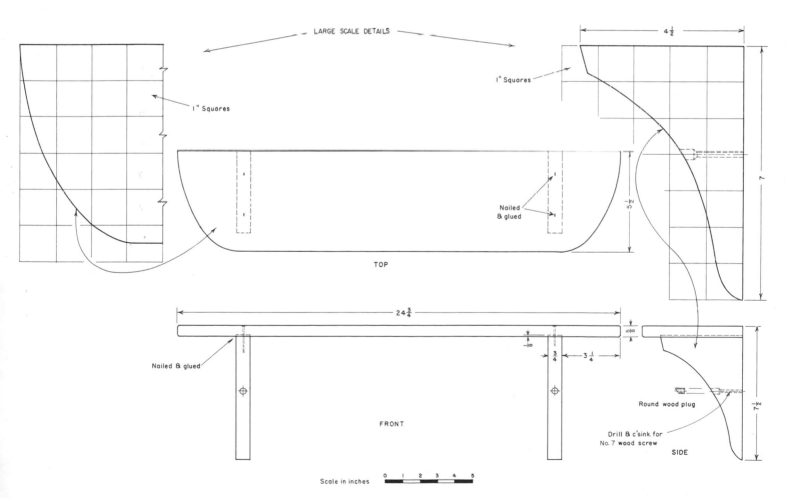

LARGE SCALE DETAILS

1" Squares

1" Squares

4½

7

5½

Nailed & glued

TOP

24¾

Nailed & glued

⅛

¾

3¼

⅝

Round wood plug

Drill & c'sink. for No. 7 wood screw

FRONT

SIDE

7½

Scale in inches

0 1 2 3 4 5

FRUITLANDS MUSEUMS, HARVARD, MASSACHUSETTS

Block Stools

These stools, similar to the low stools in the Parson Capen House, are a rarity today. At one time they were commonplace in eighteenth-century ordinaries and schools. The thick pine tops hold the wedged octagonal legs of the high stools. There is no evidence that any of these early stools had backs on them as do many contemporary "reproductions."

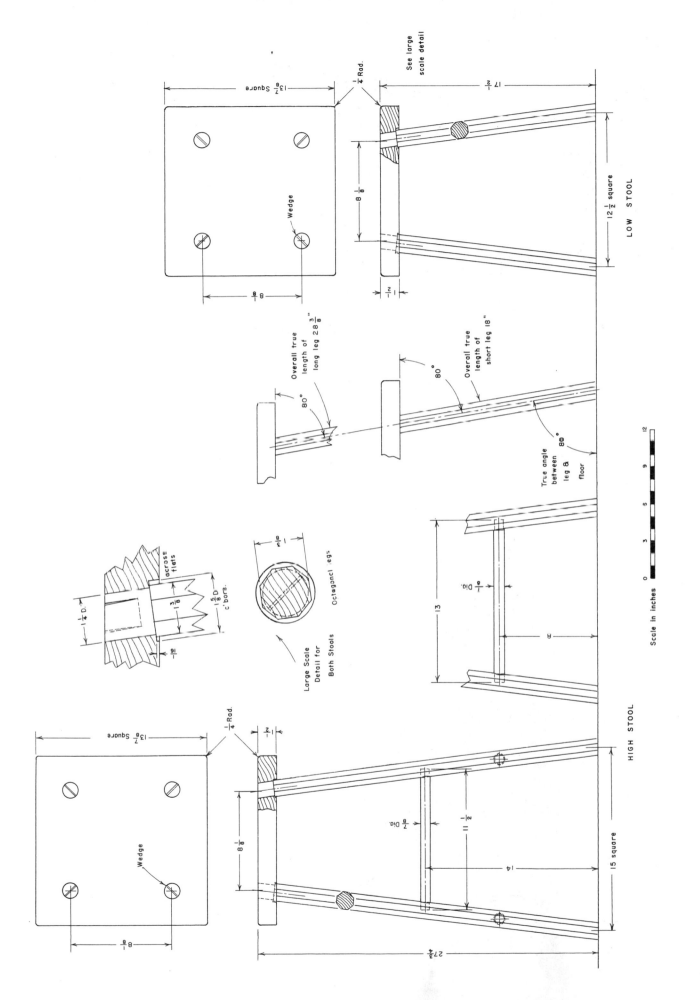

Doll's Cradle

The original of this cradle is in the Paul Revere House in Boston; it is believed to have been in the family since the American Revolution. The hood, body, and rockers are beautifully proportioned and the colonial child who tenderly placed her doll in its depths must have found great satisfaction in rocking it.

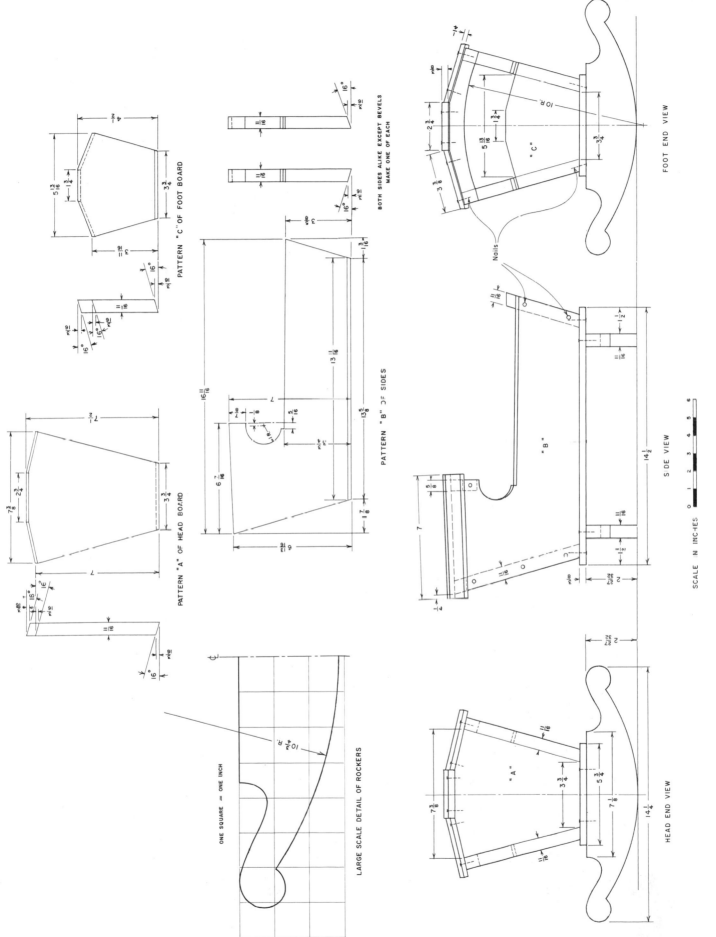

PATTERN "C" OF FOOT BOARD

BOTH SIDES ALIKE EXCEPT BEVELS
MAKE ONE OF EACH

PATTERN "B" OF SIDES

PATTERN "A" OF HEAD BOARD

ONE SQUARE = ONE INCH

LARGE SCALE DETAIL OF ROCKERS

"C"

Nails

"B"

"A"

FOOT END VIEW

SIDE VIEW

HEAD END VIEW

SCALE IN INCHES

Wayside Stand

This weaver's stand of pine and maple in the Hawthorne Room of the Wayside Inn probably had a variety of uses. According to Russell Kettell, the peculiar foot arrangement indicates that it may well have held a candle for a weaver. With the crossbar of the T base toward her, she could pass to and from her work with no danger of tripping.

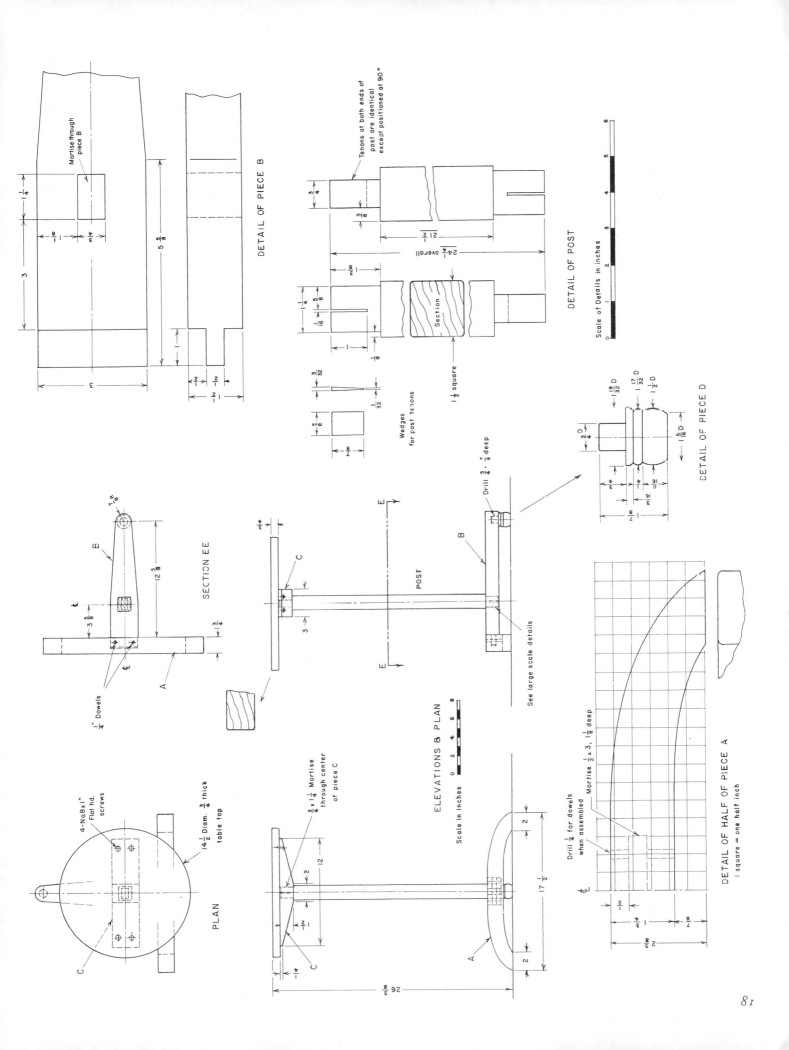

DETAIL OF PIECE B

DETAIL OF POST

Scale of Details in inches

CETAIL OF PIECE D

SECTION EE

ELEVATIONS & PLAN

Scale in inches

PLAN

DETAIL OF HALF OF PIECE A

1 square = one half inch

81

Water Bench

This unpretentious water bench is typical of the furniture found in the Plymouth area in the early 1800s. This piece from the Howland House is in the same community where the family arrived aboard the *Mayflower*. Both its "boot jack" ends and molded sides are subtle attempts at decoration. This kitchen piece held buckets of well water on its shelves before piping came into use.

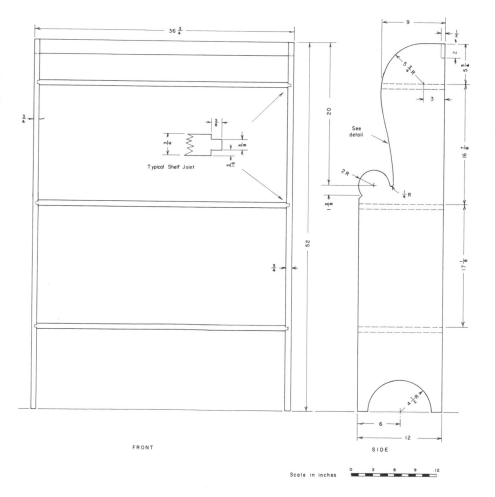

Typical Shelf Joint

FRONT

SIDE

See detail

Scale in inches

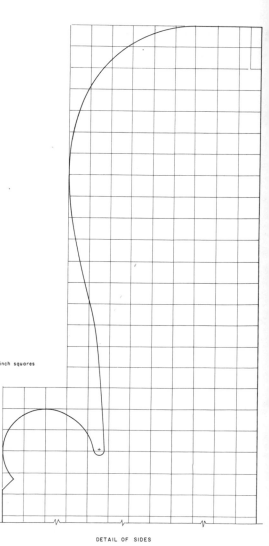

1 inch squares

DETAIL OF SIDES

Footstool

Commonly known as a five-board stool, this sturdy pine piece is in the Antiquarian Society in Concord, Massachusetts. With its graceful aprons and gothic ogee legs, this piece had a variety of uses.

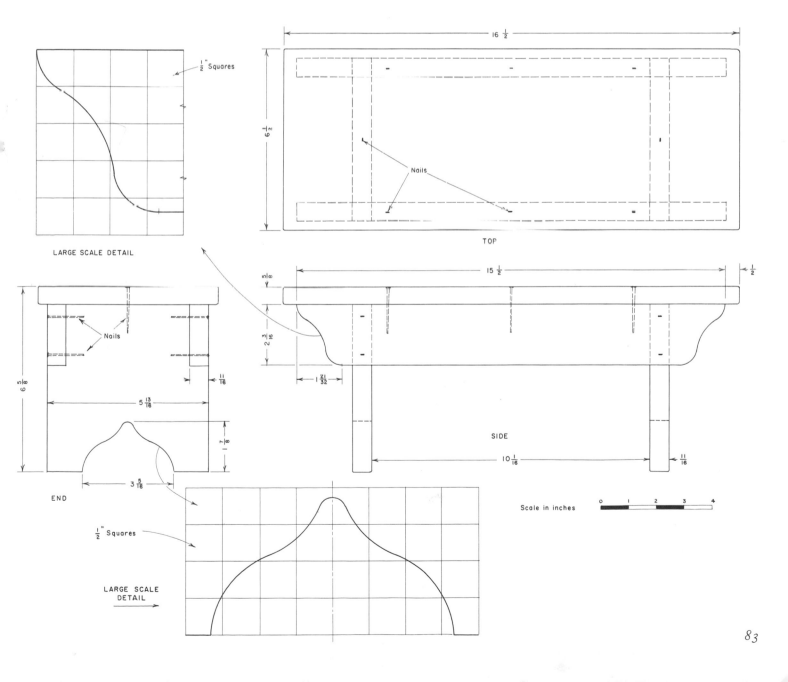

LARGE SCALE DETAIL

½" Squares

TOP

Nails

SIDE

END

Nails

Scale in inches

LARGE SCALE DETAIL

½" Squares

Settle Table

When is a table not a table? When it is a chair. Such was the eighteenth-century riddle that referred to this space-saving convertible piece. In winter its broad utilitarian top served as a dining area by the hearth. After dinner, those who warmed themselves by the fire were insulated from drafts by the same "bord" positioned vertically. Of particular interest is the curved armrest through which maple pins were inserted to hold the top securely. The storage compartment beneath the hinged seat held kindling for the fire.

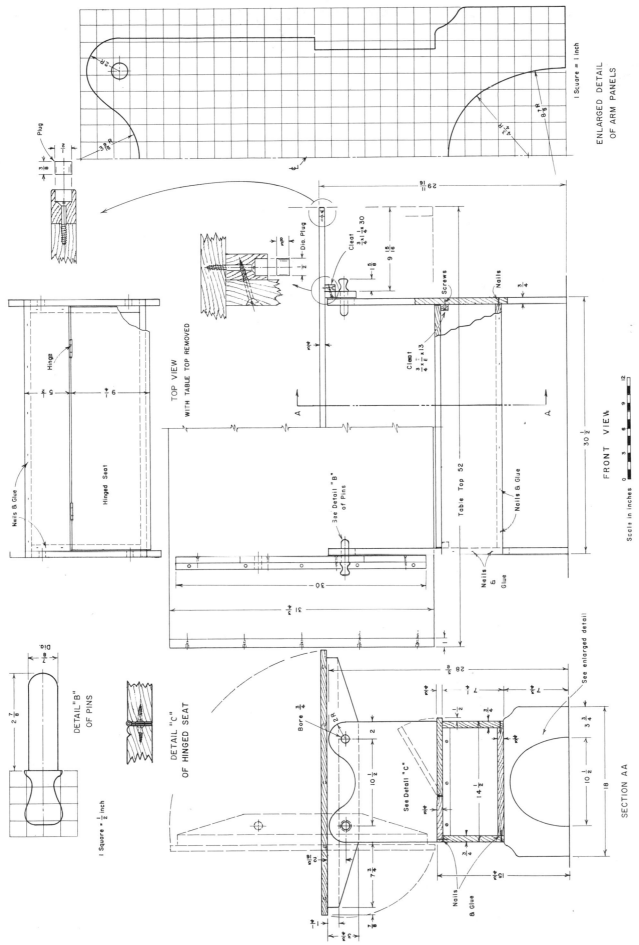

LINCOLN HOUSE, HINGHAM, MASSACHUSETTS

ENLARGED DETAIL
OF ARM PANELS

1 Square = 1 inch

TOP VIEW
WITH TABLE TOP REMOVED

FRONT VIEW

Scale in inches

DETAIL "B"
OF PINS

1 Square = ½ inch

DETAIL "C"
OF HINGED SEAT

SECTION AA

Wayside Table

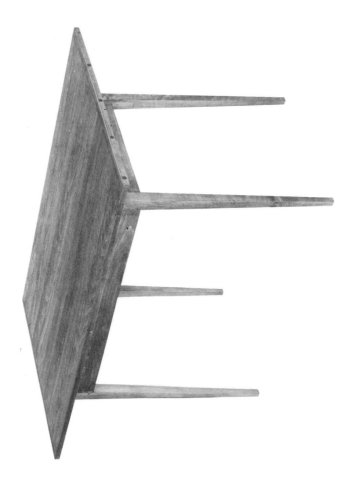

Typical of tables found in eighteenth-century hostelries, it is similar to those in use at the Wayside Inn in Sudbury, Massachusetts, and at the White Horse Tavern in Newport, Rhode Island; they were particularly in evidence in the inns along the Boston Post Road. The tops of these tables were invariably made of a "bord" of white pine. The slant legs were often made of rock maple cut into with mortises at their upper ends. These mortises supported the stretchers that, in conjunction with the legs, formed the base, or table frame. These tables were considered somewhat sophisticated in a period when most table bases had ankle-high stretchers. These contributed greatly to the strength of the tables, but were an obstacle to comfortable seating.

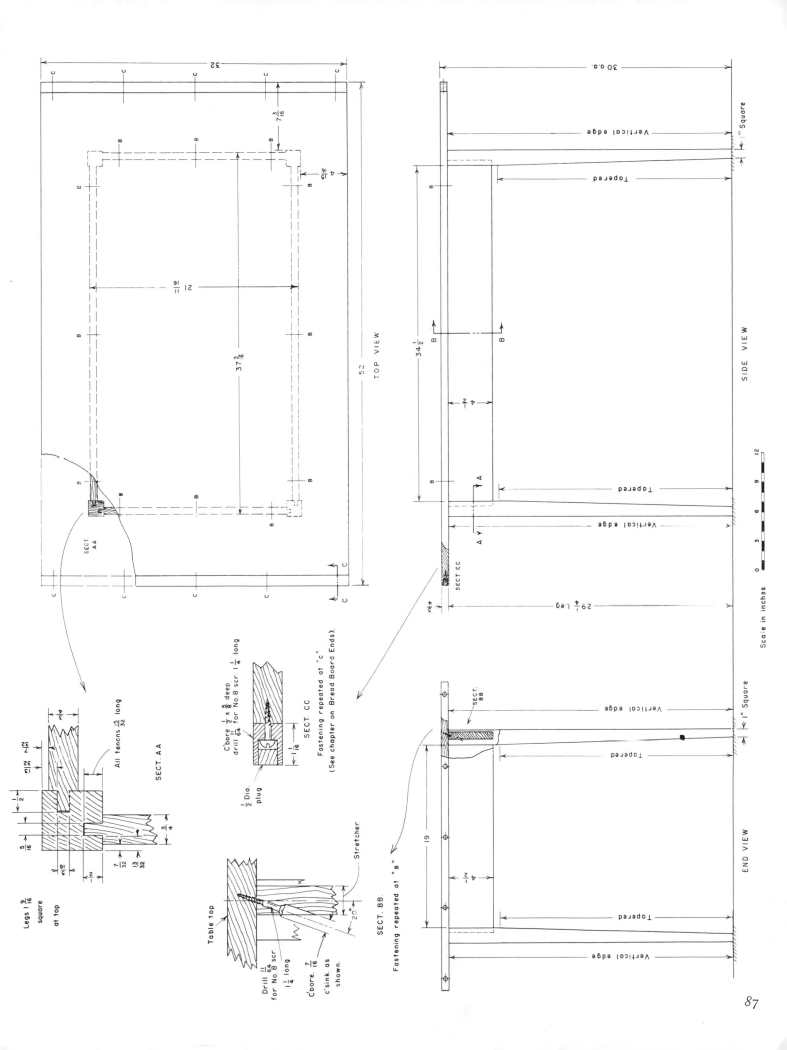

TOP VIEW

32

$7\frac{3}{16}$

$4\frac{15}{16}$

$21\frac{11}{16}$

$37\frac{3}{8}$

52

SECT. AA

Legs $1\frac{9}{16}$ square at top

All tenons $\frac{15}{32}$ long

SECT. AA

$\frac{1}{2}$

$\frac{5}{16}$

$\frac{7}{32}$ $\frac{13}{32}$

$\frac{3}{4}$

$\frac{3}{32}$ $\frac{3}{16}$

$\frac{1}{2}$

Table top

Stretcher

Drill $\frac{11}{64}$ for No. 8 scr. $1\frac{1}{4}$ long

C'bore $\frac{7}{16}$ c'sink. as shown.

2.0°

$\frac{3}{8}$

SECT. BB.

Fastening repeated at "B"

C'bore $\frac{1}{2} \times \frac{5}{8}$ deep drill $\frac{11}{64}$ for No. 8 scr. $1\frac{1}{4}$ long

$\frac{1}{2}$ Dia plug

$\frac{1}{16}$

SECT. CC.

Fastening repeated at "C"
(See chapter on Bread Board Ends).

30 o.o.

Vertical edge

Tapered

1" Square

SIDE VIEW

$34\frac{1}{2}$

$4\frac{1}{2}$

Tapered

Vertical edge

$29\frac{1}{4}$ Leg

$4\frac{3}{4}$

SECT CC

Scale in inches

0 3 6 9 12

1" Square

Vertical edge

Tapered

SECT. BB.

19

$4\frac{1}{2}$

Tapered

Vertical edge

END VIEW

87

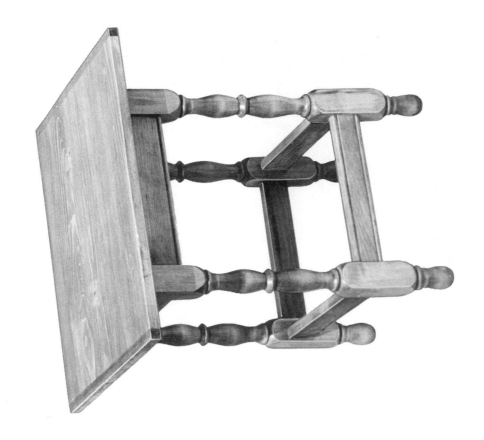

Joined Stool

Sometimes referred to as a joint stool, this piece is somewhat taller than its seventeenth-century contemporaries, which were used primarily for seating; perhaps a farmboy sat uncomfortably on its "hard" slab of pine. The term "joined" refers to the mortise and tenon joints, which were secured with dowel pins, or "tree nails." The craftsmen who built this furniture were known as "joyners," later "joiners."

The combination of woods in this piece is typical of the period, each wood being selected to serve the requirements of a particular part. A plank of pumpkin pine was used in the top, while rock maple was reserved for the delicate vase leg turnings. Today this stool serves as an occasional table.

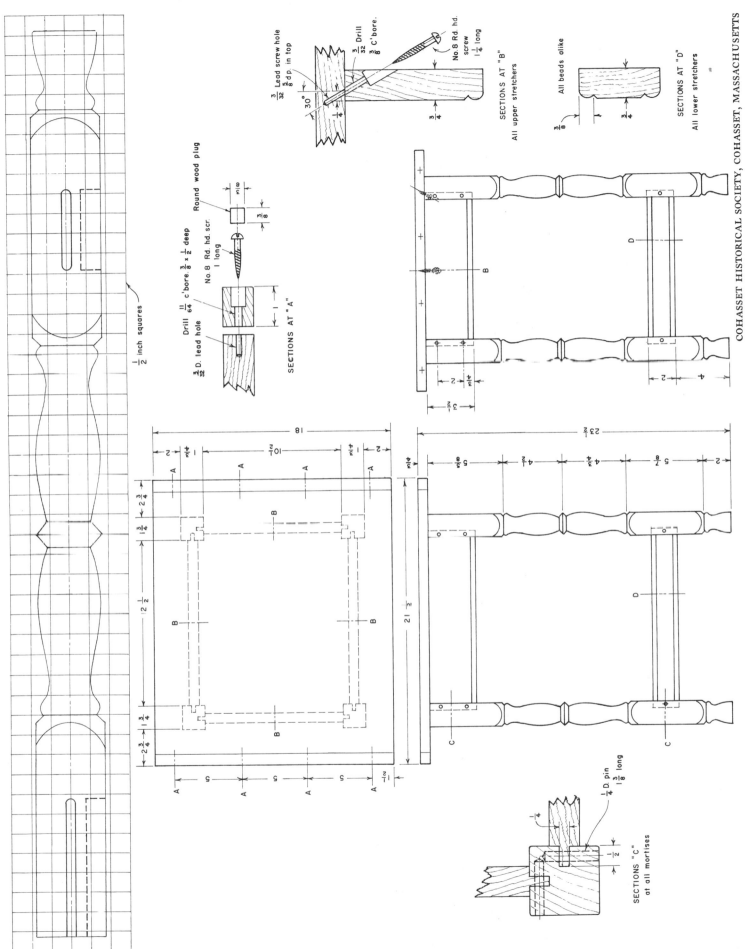

SECTIONS AT "B"
All upper stretchers

SECTIONS AT "D"
All lower stretchers

All beads alike

Round wood plug

No. 8 Rd. hd. scr.
1 long

SECTIONS AT "A"

SECTIONS "C"
at all mortises

½ inch squares

COHASSET HISTORICAL SOCIETY, COHASSET, MASSACHUSETTS

Drop-Leaf Table

Of extreme simplicity and distinction, this table gives the appearance of a modern Scandinavian import, but it is an early eighteenth-century table in the buttery of the Tavern at Old Sturbridge Village. The severity of its design strikes a sympathetic note across the centuries. Mortised and tenoned throughout, it was built for durability and the total absence of turnings indicates its use as a utilitarian piece.

Large enough to seat six people, its pine top folds to 12 inches, with the leaves almost touching the floor. It is obvious that economy of space was as important two hundred years ago as it is today.

Material pine except where otherwise noted.

TOP VIEW

Drill & c'bore for No.10 wood screws 2 long
Nails (both shelves)

Drill and C'bore for No.8 wood screws 1 3/4 long. Plug holes.

Cleat

Both gates alike
Maple

This gate shown open

SIDE VIEW

1/4 Dia. pins
Maple feet
Mortise 5/8

Plan View of Both Shelves

Drill 3/8 Dia. for hinge pins 2 holes

Typical Detail of All Joints on Both Shelves

Pin

Typical Detail of all Joints on Gates

Hinge pads 1 3/8 square

Shelf

All gate hinge pins 3/8 Dia. x 1 1/2 long
Gate leg (open)
This gate shown closed

Shelf

Mortise 5/8

END VIEW

Scale in inches
All dimensions in inches

1/4 Dia. 2 holes

91

Towne Cradle

This cradle, with its uniquely molded pine sides and maple corner posts capped with finials, is in the collection of the Essex Institute in Salem, Massachusetts. Owned originally by William Towne and his family of six, who settled in Salem sometime prior to 1635, succeeding generations, too, found security in its depth. Today, between generations, such a cradle would be quite functional holding sewing or cordwood by the hearth.

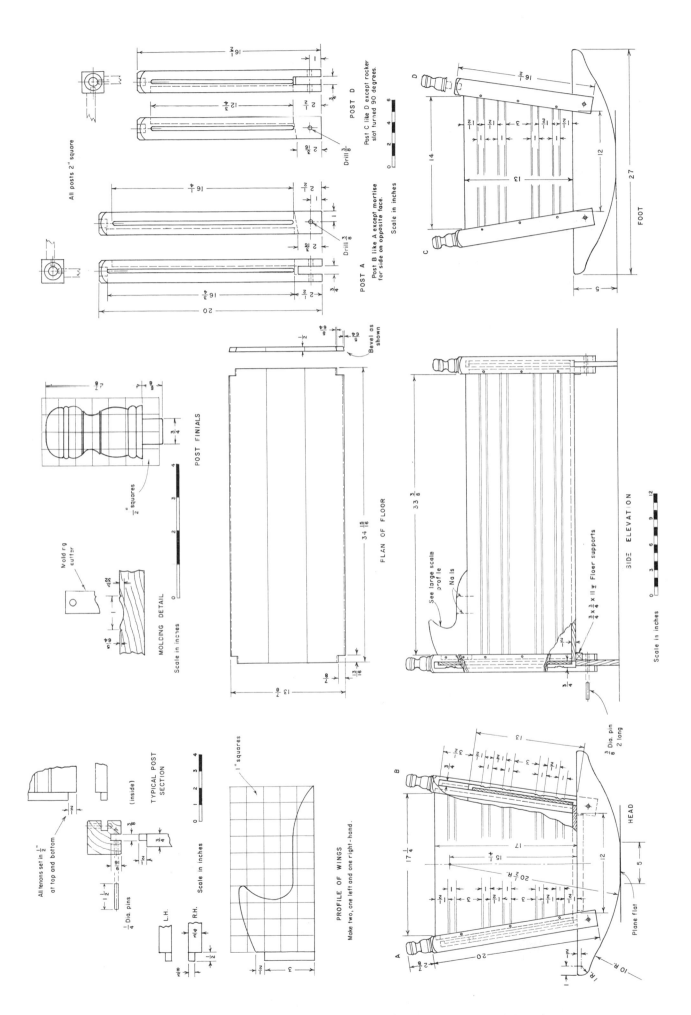

93

Schoolmaster's Desk

The desk box was a convenient place for the early settlers to keep their papers and most valuable possessions, including the family Bible. Its hinged top was slanted for convenience in writing and to hold the Bible during family prayers; a strip of molding along the front edge of the lid prevented papers and books from sliding to the floor. As years passed, a permanent frame was incorporated into the design of the box, resulting in such furniture as the schoolmaster's desk. The addition of the frame made possible the incorporation of a drawer, which held still more material. The original of this piece is in a private collection.

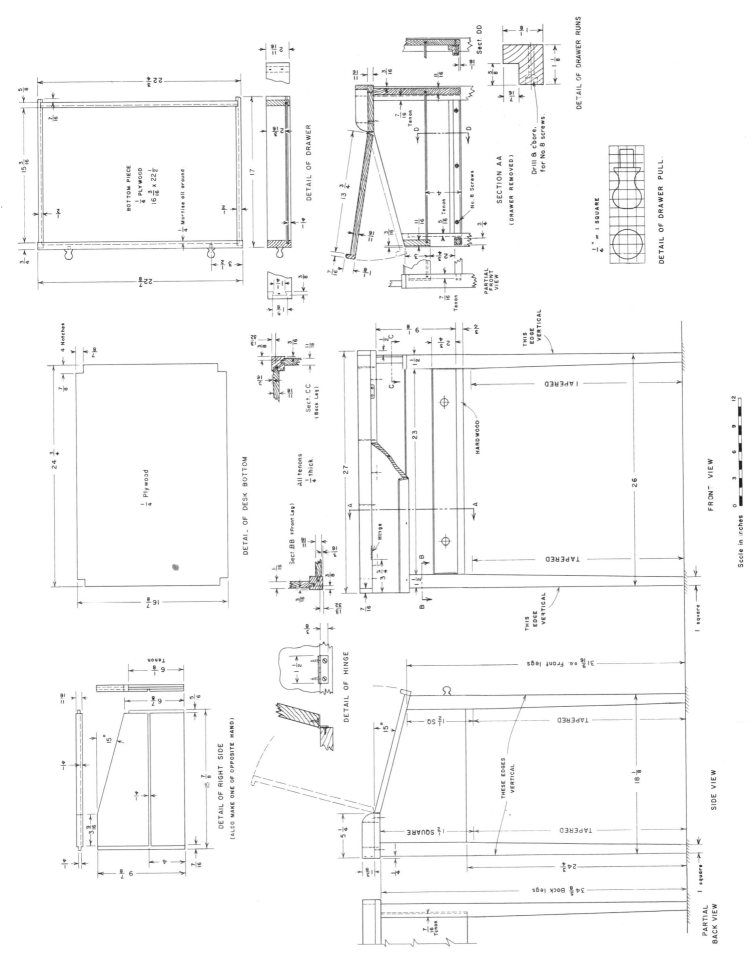

Six-Board Chest

The chest was one of the most common early furnishings. As a trunk used in travel, its hinged top kept out the dust, rain, and snow. In the home it served equally well as a storage chest, a bench, or a table. The tulip motifs and scrolled leaves in vivid colors are a clue to its Pennsylvania origin and suggest a maker's date of about 1790. This chest appears in color on the cover.

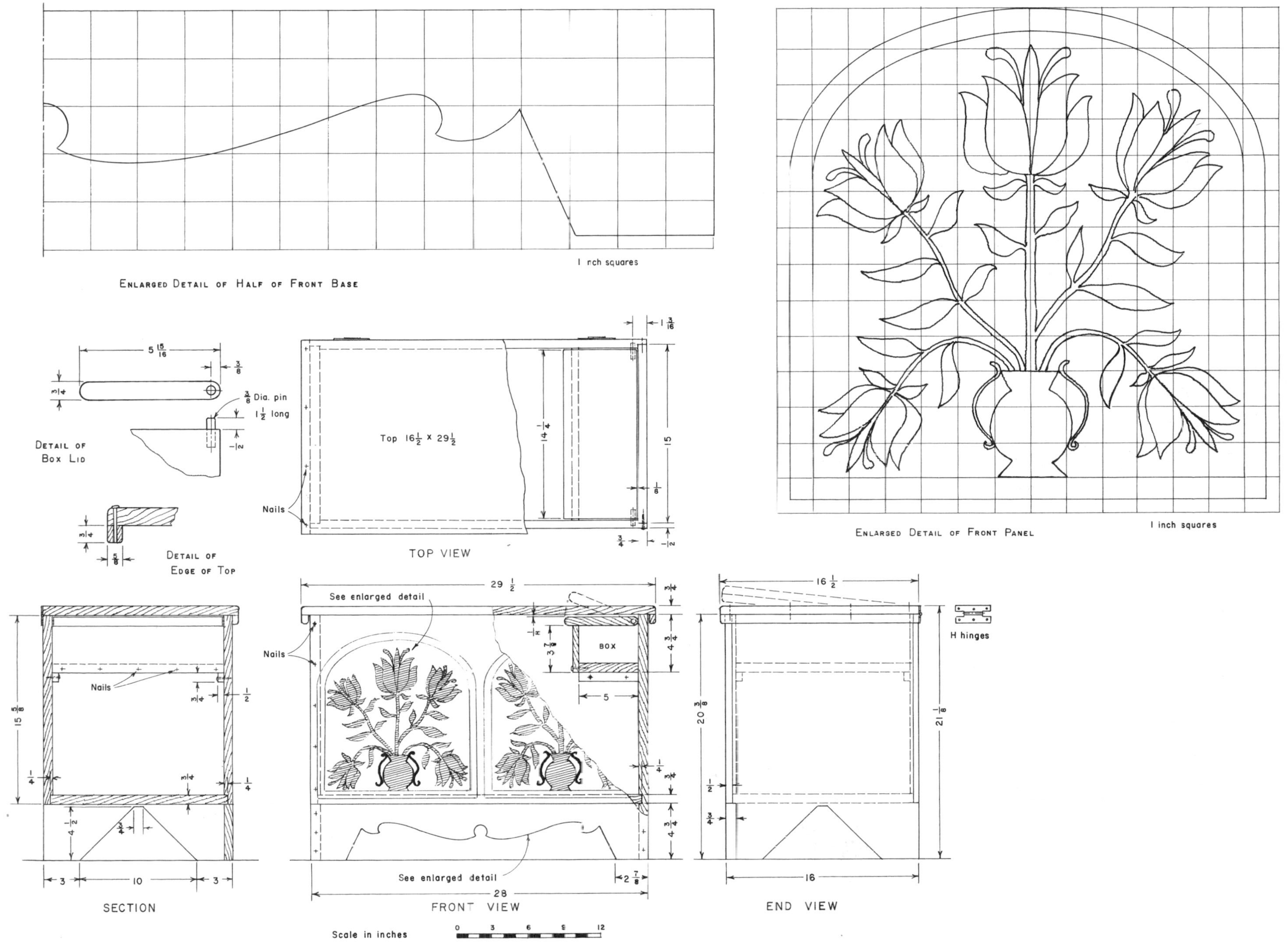

Enlarged Detail of Half of Front Base
1 inch squares
Enlarged Detail of Front Panel
1 inch squares
Detail of Box Lid
5 15/16
3/8
3/4
3/8 Dia. pin
1 1/2 long
1/2
Detail of Edge of Top
3/4
5/8
Top 16 1/2 x 29 1/2
Nails
14 1/4
15
1 3/16
1/8
3/4
1/2
TOP VIEW
29 1/2
See enlarged detail
BOX
5
3 7/8
4 3/4
28
2 7/8
See enlarged detail
FRONT VIEW
Scale in inches
0 3 6 9 12
16 1/2
H hinges
20 3/8
21 1/8
16
END VIEW
15 5/8
Nails
1/2
1/4
4 1/2
3
10
3
SECTION

New Hampshire Cupboard

This low cupboard may well have been used under the eaves in the kitchen ell of a saltbox house. In the 1700s, it undoubtedly held the everyday pewter service and treen ware. The "button" knobs on the doors add attractive focal points to the design. The original is in the collection of Mrs. Howard Abell of Milton, Massachusetts.

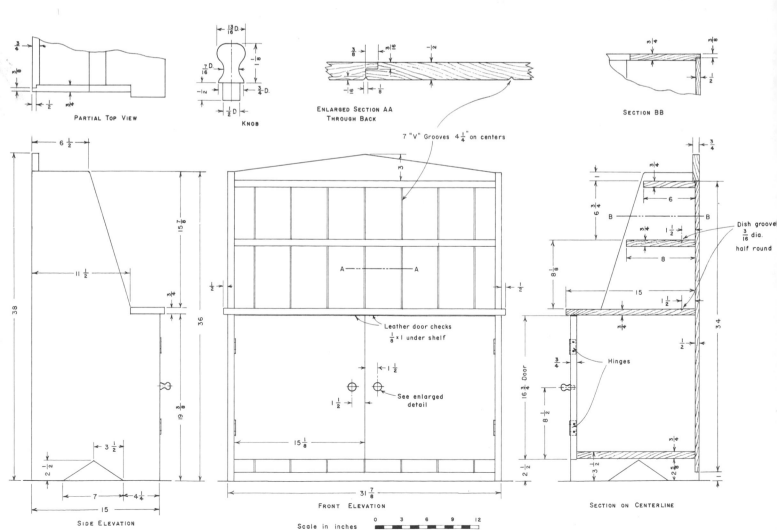

PARTIAL TOP VIEW

KNOB

ENLARGED SECTION AA
THROUGH BACK

SECTION BB

7 "V" Grooves 4¼" on centers

Dish groove
3/16 dia.
half round

Leather door checks
⅛ x 1 under shelf

See enlarged
detail

Hinges

SIDE ELEVATION

FRONT ELEVATION

Scale in inches   0   3   6   9   12

SECTION ON CENTERLINE

Stallion Weather Vane

The original of this stallion is in the barn adjacent to the Tavern at Old Sturbridge Village, Massachusetts. Its ⅞-inch-thick pine body was painted a deep red; other parts, including the "eyebrow," were painted black. If this vane is to be exposed to the weather, the board from which it is cut should be made from wood edge-glued with a waterproof adhesive. A ½-inch pipe of brass or iron should be inserted in a hole drilled in one of the front legs. This pipe gives strength to the crossgrain of the wood while at the same time providing a bearing for the supporting rod. If the horse is to be used as a wall decoration, place two screw eyes along the horizonal center line of the back, with each eye about an inch in from the end. A wire between the eyes will support the horse on a couple of wall hangers.

The horse has always been a favorite weather vane motif. This particular one is obviously proud that he has been selected to stand guard over the barn and fields as he swings at the pleasure of the wind.

I Square = I inch

¾ Pine

Free fit between
rod & tube

Both sides painted alike.

Tube inside dia.
outside dia.

PROFILE VIEW

EDGE
VIEW

⅜ Dia. rod.
tight fit

Scale in inches   0 1 2 3 4 5 6

Bull Weather Vane

The Greeks used weather vanes before the coming of Christ, but their recorded use in the American colonies goes back to about 1656, when a copper cockerel was fashioned for the Dutch Reformed Church in Albany. The majority that followed seem to be primarily farm "folk art," with attention focused on livestock. This bull, from the collection at Old Sturbridge Village, has perhaps more black spots on its white body than he would have had in reality. It represented the Holstein-Friesian breed, which has been known for its milk-producing qualities for over two thousand years. When the Dutch colonized New York, they brought their cattle with them; they were pretty well distributed throughout the colonies by 1800.

1" Squares

Black spots on white

15 x 22 Stock $\frac{3}{4}$" Thick pine.

$\frac{1}{2}$" O.D. Steel tube fixed in vane.

$\frac{3}{8}$" Dia. Rod free fit in tube.

$\frac{3}{4}$" Vane

$1\frac{1}{4}$"

PARTIAL END VIEW.

$1\frac{1}{4}$"

$\frac{7}{8}$" Dia. Collar fixed on rod.

Rod fixed in Support

Washer

Support

PARTIAL SECTION ON CENTERLINE.

Drill & C'bore. for No. 8 wood screws $1\frac{3}{4}$" long

Scale in inches

0   1   2   3   4   5

Whale Weather Vane

Whales had a special, romantic appeal to the folk artist since they conjured up stories of faraway places, and hazardous pursuit. The sperm whale, the subject of this weather vane, was the most desirable catch. He killed men and crushed the boats of those who sought him for his oil. His grim jaws make him a fearsome creature. Fighting his way into the wind, he would be an attractive addition atop any barn. The 1-inch pine body was finished in a flat black. The "cruel" teeth can best be reproduced using twentieth-century golf tees.

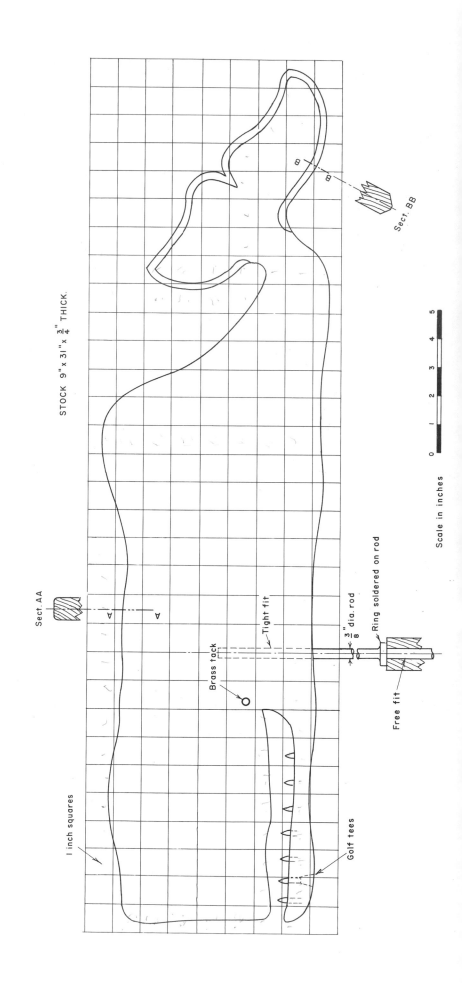

STOCK 9" x 31" x 3/4" THICK.

Sect. AA

Sect. BB

1 inch squares

Brass tack

Golf tees

Tight fit

3/8" dia. rod

Ring soldered on rod

Free fit

Scale in inches

0 1 2 3 4 5

SOURCES AND BIBLIOGRAPHY

Sources

I. TOOLS AND ACCESSORIES

Albert Constantine and Son, Inc.
2050 Eastchester Road
Bronx, New York 10461

A leading source of exotic hardwoods and veneers, picture frame moldings, furniture hardware, wood finishes, and tools.
catalogue, 50 cents

American Machine Tool Co.
Fourth and Spring Streets
Royersford, Pennsylvania 19468

Manufacturers of home workshop power tools that are relatively inexpensive and designed for light work.
leaflet, free

Brookstone Co.
Peterborough, New Hampshire 03458

Some woodworking tools, but mostly hard-to-find special small-size jewelry and machinists' tools.
catalogue, 50 cents

Craftsman Wood Service Co.
2729 South Mary Street
Chicago, Illinois 60608

Suppliers of woodworking tools and supplies plus a range of hard-to-find woods.
catalogue, 50 cents

Gilliom Manufacturing Co.
1109 North Second Street
St. Charles, Minnesota 63301

Ingeniously designed kits and plans for construction of home workshop woodworking machines. Included in the kits are all of the bearings and other metal parts needed to construct sturdy equipment. The customer supplies his own plywood and lumber.
catalogue, 50 cents

Leichtung and Galnitz, Inc.
5187 Mayfield Road
Cleveland, Ohio 44124

Sources

Catalogue shows woodworking benches, hand-forged gouges, and chisels, along with other imported hand tools.
catalogue, free

Minnesota Woodworkers Supply Co.
925 Winnetka Avenue North
Minneapolis, Minnesota 55427

A source of unique cabinet hardware, woven cane, carved finials, and upholstery tools.
catalogue, 50 cents

Silvo Hardware Co.
107–1–9 Walnut Street
Philadelphia, Pennsylvania 19106

A most worthwhile source of many tools and accessories for the home workshop including router bits, wood miter boxes, bar and pipe clamps, hand and circular saws, shoe rasps, storage bins, wood screws in steel and brass, sawhorse brackets, molding cutterheads and blades, plus hold-down clamps.
catalogue, 50 cents

The Japan Woodworker
1806 Bancroft Way
Berkeley, California 94703

Importers of fine woodworking tools, including wood-bodied block planes, chisels, gouges, and saws.
catalogue, 50 cents

Garrett Wade Company
302 Fifth Avenue
New York, New York 10001

This magnificently photographed catalogue is a compilation of all manner of imported tools including sculptor's gouges, mallets, chisels, carving knives, benchstones, and slipstones. Also exhibited are woodworking benches, vises, clamps, and mitering tools.
catalogue, $1.00

Woodcraft Supply Corp.
313 Montvale Avenue
Woburn, Massachusetts 01801

Their color catalogue displays some of the finest woodworking tools available; many are imported from sources in England and Austria where they have been produced for generations. Planes have beech bodies and hornbeam soles. They maintain a chisel- and gouge-sharpening service. Woodcraft is also a source of used antique tools such as wood-bodied planes, calipers, and spoke shaves. They also stock large-diameter bits for use with hand braces.
catalogue, 50 cents

Sources

2. TOOLS AND ACCESSORIES — STOCKING DISTRIBUTORS

General Hardware Manufacturing Co.
80 White Street
New York, New York 10013

Manufacturers of a chisel and plane-blade sharpener. They also carry circle cutters, try squares, tungsten carbide grit files, dowel centers, safety goggles, and dust masks. They request a $40 minimum charge with each order.
catalogue, free

Great Neck Tools, Inc.
Mineola, New York 11501

A source of numerous hand and power tools, including drills, chisels, hammers, levels, block planes, wooden folding rules, saws, sawhorse brackets, and bevel squares. $10 minimum charge.
catalogue, free

3. TABLE SAWS AND MOLDING HEADS

Rockwell-Delta Manufacturing Co.
400 North Lexington Avenue
Pittsburgh, Pennsylvania 15208

See the Yellow Pages under "Woodworkers' Equipment."

Sears, Roebuck and Co.
Chicago, Illinois 60607

See your telephone directory.

4. SAWGUARDS

Brett Guard, Division Foredom Electric Co.
Route 6
Bethel, Connecticut 06801

leaflet, free

Sources

D & M Guard Co.
889 Military Road
Buffalo, New York 14217

leaflet, free

General Scientific Equipment Co.
Likekiln Pike and Williams Avenue
Philadelphia, Pennsylvania 19150

leaflet, free

Mitchell Plastics, Inc.
300 North Lexington Avenue
Pittsburgh, Pennsylvania 15208

leaflet, free

Rockwell-Delta Manufacturing Co.
400 North Lexington Avenue
Pittsburgh, Pennsylvania 15208

See the Yellow Pages under "Woodworkers' Equipment."

5. MOLDING KNIVES (knives ground to shape for molding heads)

Ross Cutter and Machine Co.
265 Bear Hill Road
Waltham, Massachusetts 02154

quotations on request

6. TURNINGS (one or more of a kind)

Cohasset Woodcrafters
Attention: Bob Mattox
19A South Main Street
Cohasset, Massachusetts 02025

Sources

7. FURNITURE HARDWARE

Acorn Manufacturing Co.
Mansfield, Massachusetts 02048

A good source of black iron builder's hardware and cabinet latches.
catalogue, 50 cents

Ball and Ball
463 West Lincoln Highway
Exton, Pennsylvania 19341

A fine collection of brasses, drawer pulls, escutcheons, and bed bolt covers. Also shows fireplace screens, irons, and fireplace tools.
catalogue, $1.00

Horton Brasses, Inc.
P. O. Box 95
Nooks Hill Road
Cromwell, Connecticut 96416

An excellent source of brasses and cupboard hardware. Also, latch sets and T hinges in forged black iron. Minimum order $7.50.
catalogue, $1.00

Old Smithy Shop
P. O. Box 226
Milford, New Hampshire 03055

Latches, H & HL hinges, strap hinges, door bolts, and hand-forged hardware with flat black finish are shown. On special order, the natural "forge-worked" finish is available.
catalogue, 75 cents

Period Hardware
123 Charles Street
Boston, Massachusetts 02114

An extensive collection of drawer pulls and knobs, brass clock finials, wood turnings, cabriolet legs, balusters, spiral legs, and claw-and-ball feet. The catalogue includes posts for low beds and testers as well as finials in flame, pineapple, and urn designs.
catalogue, $2.00

Sources

Robert Bourdon
Wolcott, Vermont 05680

Here is one of the few sources left of handcrafted wrought iron latches, hinges, andirons, fireplace tools and fireplace cranes. These are all "forge-worked" as they were centuries ago.
catalogue, $1.50

8. STAINS AND PAINTS

Samuel Cabot, Inc.
One Union Street
Boston, Massachusetts 02108

leaflet, free

Cohasset Colonials
Cohasset, Massachusetts 02025

catalogue, 50 cents

Johnson Paint Co.
355 Newbury Street
Boston, Massachusetts 02115

A fine source of enamels with a flat eggshell finish mixed to match your color sample.
quotations on request

Minwax Co., Inc.
Clifton, New Jersey

leaflet, free

9. DECORATING SUPPLIES

Hammett's
Hammett's Place
Braintree, Massachusetts 02184

Includes art supplies such as bristle and sable brushes as well as a selection of carving tools and sloyd knives.
catalogue, free

Sources

Wendell Manufacturing Co.
4234 North Lincoln Avenue
Chicago, Illinois 60618

Manufacturers of wheel-tipped striping tools that enable the user to apply stripes of varying widths using oil-base paints.
  leaflet, free

10. PANTAGRAPH

Dietzen Co.
1185 Highland Avenue
Needham, Massachusetts 02194

Their no. 1880 wood pantagraph is made up of 21-inch hardwood bars with metal fulcrums for reducing or enlarging in nineteen different ratios.
  catalogue, free

Johnson Paint Co.
355 Newbury Street
Boston, Massachusetts 02115
Attention: Art Department

11. STORAGE BINS

Fidelity Products Co.
705 North Wood Avenue
Minneapolis, Minnesota 55426

  catalogue, free

Kole Enterprises, Inc.
P. O. Box 152
Biscayne Annex, Florida 33152

  catalogue, free

Sources

Langley Co.
3 Sycamore Avenue
Medford, Massachusetts 02155

catalogue, free

Material Flow, Inc.
835 North Wood Street
Chicago, Illinois 60622

catalogue, free

12. MISCELLANEOUS ACCESSORIES

Box 1776
Cohasset, Massachusetts 02025

The leaflet shows sources of wood turnings in rock maple needed to construct items shown on these pages; turnings include table legs, drawer pulls, cradle finials, and Shaker wall pegs. Also included are sources of wood stabilizer, compressed hardwood pegs, brown polyvinyl glue, reproductions of handmade nails, eastern white pine in select grades, rock maple–turning squares, and updated listings of sections 1–11 in this Source list.

leaflet, 25 cents

Author's Note

If the reader knows of additional sources of hard-to-find new tools or usable antiques, please write to Box 1776, Cohasset, Massachusetts 02025, and the word will be passed along to those interested.

Bibliography

Andrews, Edward Deming, and Andrews, Faith. *Shaker Furniture*. New York: Dover Publications, 1964.

Dry Kiln Operator's Manual. Washington, D.C.: U.S. Department of Agriculture, Forest Products Laboratory, 1961.

Emerson, George. *A Report on Trees and Shrubs in the Forest of Massachusetts*. Boston: Little, Brown, 1875.

Gardner, John. Editorials in *National Fisherman*. Camden, Maine, 1973.

Gibbia, S. *Wood Finishing*. New York: Van Nostrand Reinhold Co., 1971.

Kettell, Russell Hawes. *The Pine Furniture of Early New England*. New York: Dover Publications, 1929.

Lipman, Jean. *Folk Art in Wood, Metal and Stone*. New York: Dover Publications, 1972.

Nutting, Wallace. *Furniture Treasury*. New York: Dover Publications, 1965.

Osborn, William C. *The Paper Plantation*. New York: Grossman Publishers, 1974.

Shea, John G. *The American Shakers and Their Furniture*. New York: Van Nostrand Reinhold Co., 1971.

Sloane, Eric A. *A Reverence for Wood*. New York: Wilfred Funk, 1965.

Williams, Johns. *The Shakers and Their Inventions*. Old Chatham, N.Y.: Shaker Museum Foundation, 1957.

Wood Gluing. Columbus: Franklin Chemical Industries, 1974.